Thoughts of Yesterday

By

Catherine Frayne

Published by Book Hub Publishing
An Independent Publishing House
WestWay, Rockfield, Athenry,
Co. Galway, Ireland.
www.bookhub4u.ie

Book Hub Publishing Cover design concepts by Lubov Karpinchik. Art and design work by Lacey O' Connor. Photograph by Darius Ivan.

Frayne, Catherine, 1970
Thoughts of Yesterday/by Catherine Frayne
ISBN: 9780957562745
1.   Alzheimer's/Family Dynamics/Mental Health
2.   Health and Wellness – Ireland – Biography

BOOKHUB©

PUBLISHING

Acknowledgements

It is thanks to Dr Mary Newport that I have so many improvements to chart in this book. Her work researching Alzheimer's continues. The 300 case studies she collected have secured ongoing research with Coconut Oil in Alzheimer's at the University of South Florida Byrd Alzheimer's Institute.

Thanks to Rose McDowall of the band, Strawberry Switchblade, for allowing me to use your lyrics as I wished and for your genuine support and encouragement along the way.

Sincere thanks to my Mother's Doctor and Geriatrician.

Thanks to a loyal, kind and dedicated son who ensured Mammy took her oil every day.

Dedication

To have one 'true blue' in your life would be amazing. I have many 'true blues' in mine. And as a teacher would shout to a group of talkers at the back of the class, 'ye know who ye are yerselves!

Publisher's Note

Introduction

I have always been close to my Mother. I hold her in the highest esteem. Her dedication and devotion to her own Mother never waned through the years. She cared for my Grandmother right to the bitter end till she held that frail hand on her deathbed. Mam built her life around family, past and present. I always believed that once I had my Mother's support I could take on the world.

They say that it is only when you have children of your own do you realise how much you were loved and cared for as a child and I have to say that I see the truth in this now. She was forever on hand to give comfort and advice, the Hank Williams song, 'I Dreamed About Mama Last Night' aggregates the love and fidelity my Mother held for her family. She was that Mama who refused to let sleep come until she heard the turning of the key and knew that we were all safely in our beds.

Of course, I did not always appreciate her concern. Mornings we would gingerly open the gate and tip toe up the garden path to the sound of the birds singing, hoping against hope that sleep had overcome her. Just when we were about to sneak round the side of the house, the kitchen window would swing open and there was 'the look', which she inherited from her own mother, to bring you back down to earth with a bang. 'The look', combined with a belly full of guilt for robbing her of her badly needed night's sleep was sufficient punishment and would dissuade you from indulging in as late a night again, at least for a while anyway.

When the Alzheimer's diagnosis came I was not ready to see her catapulted into that crater of obscurity, I never will be ready for that. When I began to notice short term memory improvements in Mam I felt I was being given a second chance. Since she began to take coconut oil I feel the pause button has been pressed, some breathing space bestowed and I have grasped this time with both hands. This respite inspired me to put her stories together while she can still remember them - to write and share the journey incorporating memoirs of my mother, my friend; a lady through and through.

Chapter 1

'Where is it we are going again Catherine?' Mammy asks for the umpteenth time. 'To the hospital for your appointment Mam' I calmly respond. Oh and what's this it's for, sure there's nothing wrong with me is there?' 'Ah no, it's just a memory test Mam'. 'Oh that's right, that's grand. Aren't they taking great interest in me at my age? Thank God I don't have Alzheimer's anyway, well I'd rather lose my legs than have that', she happily announces. My heart sinks as I recall the Geriatrician's diagnosis a year ago now. 'I'm afraid your mother has Alzheimer's and the quality of her life will seriously deteriorate over the next twelve months.

As I sit in the kitchen of our farmhouse with my mother in December 2011 I note with despair that all-too-familiar vacant look in her eyes, that blankness in her expression. It's an air that I have grown to recognise and detest in equal shares. Mammy has held counsel in that chair by the range for as long back as I can remember. She was always first up in the house, ensuring her children's clothes were airing on the line. This has been her perch for more than 40 years, where she sat and advised, laughed and cried with us all. I try to make conversation but nothing seems to stimulate her interest. The air of an 80's song has been going round my head for months and as I begin to recall the lyrics I finally start to understand why this particular song resonates with me.

Just close your eyes and then remember
The thoughts you've locked away
When tomorrow comes you'll wish
You had today

And as we sit here alone
Looking for a reason to go on
It's so clear that all we have now
Are our thoughts of yesterday

If you're still here when it's all over
I'm scared I'll have to say
That part of you has gone
Since yesterday

And as we sit here alone
Looking for a reason to go on
It's so clear that all we have now
Are our thoughts of yesterday

Well, maybe this could be the ending
With nothing left of you
A hundred wishes couldn't say
I DON'T WANT TO

The song is called "Since Yesterday", and was written by Rose McDowall and performed by herself and Jill Bryson in a band they formed in Glasgow in 1981 called Strawberry Switchblade. Almost 30 years after the song was released the words conveyed exactly how I felt when I looked at my mother sitting expressionless by the range. Almost oblivious to my presence,

• • •

she responds to everything with a question and not just one question, over and over again as her life has been invaded by questions. Answers mean nothing as her short term memory fails and fades as the days go by. To look at her briefly you would never suspect a thing, but when I, her daughter, look into her eyes I see a fog, a constant look of confusion, a veil descending over the mother I knew and loved all of my life. She seems to think of nothing really, yet there is a perplexed look about her. The range runs out of fuel and goes out and she wonders why Family come and go on a constant basis but she believes she has not seen them for a long time. She holds a tissue in her hand which she winds repeatedly until eventually shreds break off and fall to the floor, an action which I feel is symbolic of how we are losing a Mammy bit by bit by bit.

My mother was diagnosed with Alzheimer's two years previously. The illness progressed rapidly, in my opinion, and the outlook was devastating. Even before Mammy was diagnosed, I felt a subtle separation occurring between us, a distraction and vagueness seeping into her very soul. The lifelong close bond we shared seemed to be shaken by the onset of Alzheimer's.

I would be lying if I did not admit that I wanted to stay away so that I would not have to watch her slide fast into an unreachable world. Every part of me ached with grief at the loss I was feeling. This loss, I compared to that of a missing person, because as I sat beside her it felt as if we were miles and miles apart. Through persistent evaluation, hope, against my better judgement, got in the way of grieving. The medical Specialist who diagnosed Mammy's condition said "Your Mother has a rapid form of Alzheimer's and the quality of her life will seriously deteriorate

* * *

over the next year". I did not dare to imagine how accurate his prognosis would be. But, before I continue and before you decide that you know which way this story is going, bear with me. This story has, indeed, a very sad beginning, but I could not be more content with the fact that this book does not have an ending in the conventional sense. Instead, the ending is on-going and in a most unanticipated and heart-warming way.

Allow me to take you back in time in order to introduce you to the lady who is at the centre of this beautiful story, my Mother, an iron lady with a heard of solid gold, a most honourable woman whom you could trust with your life till the far end of time.

Mammy was born in the early 1930's to a family who were to be tainted by loss after loss, as most families at the time were. By the mid 1930's my grandparents were blissfully proud and protective of their remaining four little girls. Five babies died as a result of miscarriages and stillbirths. In the 1930's, stillborn babies were not permitted to be buried in consecrated ground as they had not yet been baptised by a Catholic priest. And so, these little infants were taken to a field known as "An Gharidín", not far from my grandparents' house, where before the morning light hit the sky, they were buried - nameless in the cold morning soil. No headstones to acknowledge their birth or brief existence on this earth, no flowers or priests prayers to accompany them to the next world.

Neither Grandma nor Granddad, ever discussed their lost children yet they never failed to pass An Ghairdín without making the sign of the cross whilst beating their hearts in private acknowledgement of the babies that had never come to live out their lives on this Earth

When Mammy was 6, herself and her sister Anna who was 2 years younger caught bad colds and were confined to bed. Anna developed pneumonia, and her gravely worried parents took her to the Doctor. Penicillin and Sulphonamides were prescribed and a twenty four hour vigil had to be maintained in order to keep her temperature down. Granddad, a skilled carpenter who once made his own violin, decided to make a miniature medicine cabinet to house Anna's medications. He set about this task not only armed with all the necessary carpentry tools, but with a heart full of hope for his little girls recovery. When Anna's fever worsened during the night, her parents were faced with the harrowing decision of whether to lift Anna from her warm bed, saddle up the horse and trap and take her out into the cold night air to be seen by the Doctor, who lived several miles away, or to hope and pray that their little girl would make it through the night. The outcome of the judgement they made that night, to leave their little angel in the warmth of her bed, while trying to take down the fever, would go on to torment and haunt them for the rest of their days.

As the cruel light of dawn crept through the bedroom window, a broken-hearted mother, wrapped in a jet black shawl, stood at her children's beds and with a cry that came from the very depth of her soul, broke the news, "Poor Anna is gone".

At 83, Mammy still vividly recalls that morning and cries deeply when she pictures her distraught mother standing at the end of her bed. She also remembers seeing the tiny coffin being brought into the bedroom, as she lay still confined to her room, while

• • •
5

little Anna's body was taken from the bed opposite and laid in the coffin to be taken away forever. Mammy also recalls the childish innocence of her thinking at the time as she wondered "Maybe I will be allowed out of bed so today". Children can be greatly shielded from the horrors of reality by the selfishness and lack of ego development which outlines their age. Unlike her siblings in An Ghairdín, Anna was allocated a plot all to herself in the sanctuary of consecrated grounds in the local graveyard. Anna, after all, had lived long enough to be baptised.

And so the family of six had now become five, and as they walked from the graveyard on that bitterly cold morning in March 1937, something deep inside Granddad broke away, his spirit, a fragment of his heart, whichever it was, he left it inside the gates of the graveyard that morning, never again to be retrieved. He took this unresolved grief to his own grave with him where, years later, he would be finally reunited with his daughter in the family plot.

Grandma battled on, as most mothers do, but a part of Granddad died with Anna that night and to balance that loss he gained feelings of self-blame, anger guilt and despair. He returned to his home that day with the emptiness of having one less tiny mouth to feed, one vacant bed, a cabinet of medicine which was no longer required. Ultimately, it left him without hope or purpose.

Grandma appeared, at least on the surface, to be better armed to cope with loss and grief, that is not to say that the same feelings of sadness and desolation did not burn inside her, but there was a practicality and hardness to the fore, a sideways glance which saw three remaining little girls looking up at her, needing to be fed, clothed and sent to school. She still had three children who desperately needed a Mammy to rear them.

Chapter 2

On Mammy's first day at school, she walked hand and hand with her older sister. Along the way a girl called Jackie came out of her house, took a look at my mother and declared "I'll be your friend" as she grabbed Mammy's free hand. And friends they became and stayed for many decades. School days for Mammy were mostly fraught with terror of their teacher, Miss O'Connor who frightened the life out of every child she taught. She and her sisters raced bare foot the 3 miles to school for fear of being late, and sat in damp clothes for the day after usually getting soaked from rain on the way.

They were forced to face the humiliation of being branded "potato pickers" by Miss O'Connor after Mammy and her sisters returned having had to take a day or two off school to help their Father on the farm because the brothers they'd had lay at peace in An Ghairdín.

The stick would be waved over her head for "not learning" arithmetic when, in truth the neurons in her brain were frozen with terror and only began to thaw as the school day came to an end. In those days, families had to take it in turns to bring in their share of turf for the fire, those who did not have ample reserves of turf had to pay a half crown. Students were sent to fetch water from the well for the teacher's lunch time tea. Mammy always said she would like to have come to meet Miss O'Connor years after she left school, but only because she wanted to slap her face in return for the years of fear and trauma she inflicted on her, her siblings and classmates.

To compensate for the horror of the class room, Mammy and her sisters would try and knock as much fun out of the walk home from school as they could. They picked and ate berries from the brambles and when the season was right they helped themselves to a turnip from the field and ate it raw. No great deadline or fear had them hurrying home, so they used this time to socialise, tease and torment whoever they came across along the way.

The first port of call would be a stone wall, over which they would lean and watch a farmer and his sons plough the field. Mammy remembers how one of the sons once brought over the horse to the wall and asked them to smile so that he could take their photo. Delighted to be asked, Mammy and her sisters happily obliged as they grinned broadly in anticipation of the camera's appearance. The young lad reversed the horse up to the stone wall, lifted the horse's tail and shouted "smile". The girls would fall about laughing and, with tears streaming down their faces, race home to tell their mother about the famous camera in the field.

Ms Moloney lived alone in a cottage which the girls passed en route from the school. The widow's door was always open and the girls welcomed the opportunity to go in and 'draw out' the lady. They would bombard the poor widow with ridiculous questions which they repeated over and over without stopping to give the poor woman a chance to answer. Ms Moloney would ask them what they learned in school that day and they would make up the greatest nonsense they could think of in reply. Eventually, she would tire of their senseless chat and let a roar at them, "Get off with ye now". As they skipped out the door the last thing they would hear her shout was, "Well thank God there isn't any more of ye in it". Never one to take offence, Grandma merely laughed when they told her what Ms. Moloney had said.

Grandma, along with most housewives in the 1930's, had her own meagre income by means of selling eggs that her hens laid. As there was no Children's Allowance to be claimed at the time, most women kept a valued flock of hens, the income from which, they heavily relied on. Essentials, such as flour and sugar, were bought with the proceeds. This "egg money" was at all costs to be kept hidden from the man of the house who might take a notion to spend it in the pub. Hens were put into a box to hatch or 'clock' in the spring. Ten to twelve eggs would be put under the 'clocker'. The 'clocker 'had to be kept away from other hens at this time in case any of the eggs got broken. After a week or two Grandmas would light a candle and hold the egg up to it to see if it had a chicken forming. If she could make out a blackness inside then it was an earner, if not it would be discarded. After three weeks the chicks would begin to hatch and emerge. They were fed on oatmeal until they were hardy enough to run around and needed to be fed four times a day.

On Thursday every week the "Eggler" would call in his van. The egg man bought the eggs and offered payment of either cash or groceries in return. There was great excitement in the home the day the "Eggler" was due. As he drew up to the house the girls raced out after grandma almost sending her flying with the basket of eggs. The egg man not only sold bare essentials but sweets as well and there was always the chance that Grandma would splash out on a few clove drops or biscuits out of her precious earnings.

• • •

Grandad was by now well lost to a life of self-blame and remorse. He threw himself into helping everyone he could in the village albeit to the exclusion of his own family. He began to document every birth, death, marriage and immigration in the surrounding area. He recorded cures he learned of, for all types of ailments both in humans and in animals. He rarely talked in the house but read incessantly. Where death was imminent in a home, Granddad would be called on to sit with the dying.

Through time and experience Grandad was able to accurately determine exactly how long the chronically ill had to live. He became a great comforter to those who were passing, and as a result gave solace to the immediate family. Mammy well remembers the numerous mornings she watched her Father return, ashen faced, having spent yet another night by a deathbed. Regardless of the number of brows Grandad wiped as they slowly moved towards the light and into another world, no hand or brow would ever feel as soft and tender than that of his own beautiful daughter, Anna.

Chapter 3

Mammy was never afforded the opportunity to attend secondary school, the reason being that she and her sisters were required to work on the farm for their early teenage years, given that there was no son to take the reins and work alongside Granddad. Basic education in the 1940's was provided to the mass of the population by a system of Church-controlled State-supported National Schools, the vast majority of which were one or two-teacher schools. Many pupils did not complete their primary education and few went on to second level.[1]

Saving the turf was a lengthy process. Long sunny days of the summer were spent in the bog with Granddad. He would cut the turn himself with a sleán before firing it out of the bog hole to an area where it would dry. The girls would have to be up and out of bed very early on those long sunny summer days. Grandma would have lunch prepared and ready to go, a glass bottle of tea wrapped in newspaper, freshly made brown bread with a scraping of butter melted into it and an egg if times were good. The ass and cart transported Granddad and the girls to the bog where the first important job was to leave the basket of food in the shade. The cart was taken off the ass and he was left to entertain himself as he grazed on the meagre offerings of the bog land. As Granddad cut, Mammy and her sisters would gather the turf and make it into gróigíns. They provoked each other by

---

[1] Ref That was then, This is now Change in Ireland, 1949-1999. Central Statistics Office (published & produced) (Publication to mark the 50th anniversary of the CSO, edited by Adrian Redmond copyright Government of Ireland 2000.

• • •

firing Ciarán's (little pieces of turf) when no one was looking. They couldn't wait to get the nod from Granddad that it was time for lunch. Once the signal was given, off they would race in search of a clump of heather growing on a dry hummock. Out came the bottle of tea which tasted sweeter than they could have imagined as it warmly washed down the buttered bread. Mammy can still close her eyes and recall the tastes which were handsomely complimented by the subtle scent of heather mixed with the unique fragrance of the unpolluted bog air. After eating they would spend a while exploring, looking for frogs, picking cotton balls and squeezing soft lumps of turf between their fingers as they made imaginary iced cakes out of the flora and fauna they found. As the evening drew in the girls celebrated with glee the much anticipated signal to go home.

While Granddad was reintroducing the ass to the cart the girls were soaking their sore and tired feet in the ice cold water of a nearby bog hole, wearily yearning for their beds. Once the turf had sufficient time and weather to dry, usually a few weeks, it was transported home and made into a reek in the shed in preparation for winter.

My Grandparent's home was always open and welcoming for visitors regardless of the time of day or night. Visitors were given the best seat in the house, the plinth beside the big open fire. Mammy and her sisters would greatly resent this as they were usually scuttled away from the fire to make way for the guests or hunted off to bed for fear they would hear any local chat or gossip. Oh, how they longed to sit up at the fire like the grown-ups, enjoying the heat and highly entertaining stories that were being told. Visitors were hardly seated when Grandma would have the kettle on, she would then go to the dresser and take out one of her home made cakes and cut off a big thick chunk and lather it with homemade butter. One visitor was known for having his long arm outstretched to accept the bread well in advance of Grandma having even left the dresser.

Ghost stories were virtually an epidemic at the time. Granddad's firm belief was that there were spirits going around as thick as blades of grass and by thick he meant plentiful! No claimed sighting was ever dismissed by Granddad. Ironically, the most frequently claimed glimpses were on the road right beside An Ghairdín where most of the babies from the village lay in rest.

By definition a ghost was a big shadow of a man either on a horse or a bicycle who passed in the night without uttering a word to anyone he met. One night, a visitor called Johnny, had himself half scared to death relaying ghost stories to Grandma and Granddad. He got up and put on his coat to leave. Granddad bid him goodnight and slipped out the back door when Johnny was not looking. Once outside, he put on his overcoat back to front and pulled up the collar. He took off on his bicycle. As Johnny was cycling away from the house, Granddad turned back and cycled towards him, whizzing past without uttering a word. He could almost hear Johnny's knees shake as he hit the pedals with the terror flowing through him. The following night Johnny burst into Granddad's and with his fear still palpable, relayed the story of his encounter with a ghost the night before. Granddad listened intently, nodding in agreement that Johnny had indeed encountered yet another ghost.

As Mammy and her sisters got older they became, as is natural, interested in lads. They spent their summer evenings chatting and joking with boys at the crossroads. Grandma would not allow

● ● ●

herself be seen to approve of the meetings so she would throw on her shawl and walk towards the crossroads, stopping short yet close enough for the girls to see her. She never needed to say a word as 'the look' was a sufficient 'fear-inducer'. With blushes that rose from their toes, the girls would make their excuses and race off home before the scarlet embarrassment had reached their faces. Eventually, the girls had Grandma's permission to go to the dances. Excitement and apprehension built up from Monday morning until the dance on Sunday evening.

Granddad, on the surface, did not give approval for the girls to go dancing and so the preparations had to be done in secret. Mammy and her sisters would bid goodnight to their parents and go upstairs to get ready with what little clothes and makeup they had. They would slip out the bedroom window and land on the flat roof of the scullery, hopping off and racing down the road as fast as their legs would carry them. In truth, they knew that Granddad was aware of the great Sunday night escapes, but by keeping his silence, he was absenting himself from any blame, should anything happen to his girls.

From the crossroads they could hear the music already luring them. In through the dance hall doors they would burst with plumes of thick woodbine smoke bellowing out to greet them. Touring bands blasted out the music and entertainment. Most of the early dance halls did not have electricity or a PA system and so the band member's car batteries were used by the musicians for amplification. It was compulsory for neighbour lads to offer dances and great offence would be taken should a girl refuse, equal umbrage was taken should a lad you knew not invite you out for a dance. It was an almighty compliment to be offered a mineral and the only thing that would surpass that was to be offered a seat home on the crossbar of the lads bicycle! Prospects rose higher again if he offered you a pull of his fag. Cloud nine in the 1940's was the crossbar of a bicycle on a starry night with little but the red top of a cigarette to light the way home. And with flattened curls, smudged and faded make up, the stench of woodbines off their clothes, Mammy and her sisters would climb back up onto the scullery roof and hop into their beds, heavy hearts telling them that it would feel like forever before Sunday came round again.

Chapter 4

Prospects were poor for a girl in the 1940's unless she married herself to a lad with a farm. Mammy's older sister had no desire to commit to this lifestyle having worked her fingers to the bone for little return on her father's farm and so she took the brave decision to immigrate to America. Emigration was comparable to death at that time as there was little chance that those who left would ever return. Mammy was heartbroken and out of this came her determination to hold onto her younger sister and discourage her from following that same path. Mammy's strong-willed little sister was not to be convinced and so she took herself off to Birmingham without telling a soul. The first her family heard of it was when they received a letter with the British postmark from Maureen, saying that she was settling into life in England and had landed herself a job with the bus transport company, Midland Red. Mammy and Grandma were hot on her heels and arrived in Birmingham to locate and bring Maureen home. They hopped onto a big red bus in Birmingham and readied their money as the conductress approached. They could hardly believe their eyes when they saw that the conductress was their very own Maureen!

With great work they got her to come back home with them. Mammy, who was working herself at the time, offered to pay for Maureen to study nursing in Dublin. Sadly, Maureen refused the offer, the world was still her oyster, and first chance she got she took herself off to join her oldest sister in New York.

Needless to say, my mother was devastated. Hopes of holding onto her young sister were well and truly dashed. Mammy often told me that she would have loved to join her sisters in the States, but the responsibility to stay and care for her aging parents weighed heavily on her. So she denied herself the dream and took up a job in a nearby town where she would be on hand to look after her mother and father. She bought herself a German 3 wheel car so that she could visit her parents regularly. Someone then warned her that if she ever had a crash in the little car she would never survive it, so she gave up driving and bought herself a bicycle instead.

She would often finish work after 8pm in the evening and cycle the fourteen miles to see her parents and bring them the essentials they needed. She bought tins of paint, carried them the fourteen miles on the handlebars of her bicycle, painted rooms, then left at 6 am in the morning to cycle all those miles again in order to arrive at work on time. A local Pharmacist often noted Mammy taking off for the long journey laden with groceries piled into bags on the handlebars, and he would comment, 'Well, there wouldn't be a God in it if you don't have luck for the way you look after your parents'. Irrespective of the weather Mammy cycled the twenty eight mile round trip home.

On Sundays Mam would cycle to her parents in the afternoon with the makings of a nice dinner. Grandma did not really leave the house often to go shopping, and so as a result, she was totally reliant on her husband to bring home the necessities. Granddad often got intercepted by a pub on his way home so Mammy felt it her sense of duty to keep her mother stocked up with the basics essentials she may at times be waiting on. Mammy's heart would heave as Grandma waved her off into the distance, once she was

• • •

out of sight though Mammy began to picture the shining lights of the dance hall on that Sunday evening and by the time she got back to the big town her enthusiasm for dancing had helped somewhat to ease the pangs of loneliness.

Mammy spent twelve happy years working, socialising and dancing. Her duty to her parents never slumped or suffered not even when she met and married my Father. She reared four children while welcoming on board her Mother-in-Law who had no one to live with, until the lady passed away four years later. Mammy was pregnant with her fifth child in the summer of 1973 when her own Father died. Telephones were a luxury not afforded to homes at the time. News of a death therefore had to be delivered by telegram. And so, for all the death bed brows he soothed, for all the thirsty lips he moistened and for all the ebbing hands he reassuringly held, Granddad slipped gently away to the next world all alone in a hospital bed.

Not long after Granddad's death Mammy sent for Grandma to come and live with us. I was born three years earlier, the second youngest in a family of five. I had not remembered much of what Grandma was like prior to her arrival so I was so excited to think we had a replacement Grandma in such a short space of time.

I can still see her standing at the door on the cold and dark autumn evening she arrived. She looked so lonely and insecure. She was wearing a black wool coat and hat and had a brown leather suitcase gripped tightly in her hand, the smell of mothballs rising off her. I knew what mothballs smelled like but I had no idea how they looked until I found one in Grandma's

● ● ●

pocket and popped it into my mouth!! I lost my trust in mints for a good long time after that! I'm sure my Grandmother felt that her daughter had more than enough on her plate with having five children to rear, but she also had tasted loneliness and knew it to be a fate worse than death. She tried to make her presence in the house as imperceptible as possible, mainly staying in her room and only coming up to tidy the house while we were all gone to mass. She must have had something against sweeping brooms because she always used a cloth or tissue to sweep the floor. I spent many Sunday afternoons rummaging in the dustbin for dolls and toys she would have thrown out while we were at mass. Anything left on the floor was fair game for Grandma and it was consigned to the bin. In hindsight, it was a very good lesson for us. Following a few harsh losses we began making it our business to tidy up before mass valuing our toys far too much to allow them in the bin. This delighted my mother no end.

Grandma snored like nothing I had ever heard in my short life before. We had to take it in turns to sleep in the single bed in her room in case she got up and fell in the middle of the night. I was so young, I thought snoring was a ghost and my brother amplified my fear by confirming that the sound of snores actually came from a ghost. I would hardly sleep a wink when it was my turn to play night-watchman over Grandma, partially suffocated for the hours of darkness, with the blankets pulled rigidly around my head. Mummified and paralysed with fear, I couldn't wait for the morning to dawn. Grandma kept her handbag on her bed at all times, accompanied by a bottle of orange and a packet of plain biscuits. She was always generous in sharing her treats, a slug of the sticky orange drink was vital for washing the dry biscuit down.

• • •

There was always a silver tin resting on Grandma's bed, the contents of which were never proffered. 'Never mind', was all she would say when we asked what the tin contained. Our minds boggled but not for long, we watched our chance till Granny went to the kitchen and sneaked a look. We could smell the chocolate before the lid was fully unscrewed, prospects began to look even better once when we saw the tiny grains of flaky dark brown chocolate inside, we threw back mouthfuls of the newly discovered treasure before replacing the lid and leaving the tin back beside Grandma's handbag. Mammy couldn't fathom how we all got the runs in synchronicity that night, neither could we, until years later when we were told that the legendary tin which Grandma closely guarded on her bed contained maximum strength laxatives!

I can still picture the pale blue and pink high necked jumpers she wore, the cosy wool cardigans and the way she sat in the armchair, one fist closed with her thumb sticking out. She had lovely soft skin with kindly features and she wore a pair of big brown wide-rimmed glasses. As she got older she refused to have a colour put in her hair. We took it in turns to wash her locks over the bath. 'Oh hurry up me back is broken', she complained as we tried to quickly sneak the colour into her hair. My own back is breaking too I used to think but never say. 'What's that you're putting in now, I thought you had it rinsed, it better not be that Grecian 2000. I told you I don't want any colour in my hair'. She didn't miss a trick.

She told us stories and taught us how to say our prayers. 'No, not Haily Mary. It's HAIL Mary', I can still hear her cry. She got a new chair for her room and we tormented her for turns to sit and swing off it. 'Mind, would ye knock it over', she'd shout. We

• • •

wondered why she was so afraid of a chair falling over until we lifted the seat one day to discover a pot. The much sought after chair was quickly abandoned once we discovered it was a commode!

Grandma held strong opinions and beliefs with regard to how women should behave, which was compliant with her own up-bringing and the era in which she was born. I remember showing her a picture of The Little Mermaid in Copenhagen as I went over my Geography homework one evening; she declared in disgust that "that lady would want to be scorched with a nettle for exposing herself in public like that"!

As the years went on Grandma developed the condition which was then written off as 'seafóid', in today's term that would have be diagnosed as Alzheimer's. It appeared to ascend on her overnight but then we were seeing her every day so it was difficult for us realise, that the symptoms had, in fact, snuck up on her over time.

She developed all of the classic symptoms that her own daughter would go on to experience in time. Disorientation to time and place, Granny kept asking to go home. She misplaced everything without any recollection what so ever. Her mood, behaviour and personality changed and she developed a great sense of distrust. Her cheerful greeting when I would come to sit on her bed and chat changed to a suspicious shout 'What do YOU want?' She always had a coin for you on your birthday; you would hardly have your special day announced, when the gold clasp on the black leather handbag was opened. 'Let me see now have I anything for you', she would say reaching deep into the bag. As her own dementia deteriorated her impatience increased. 'It's my birthday tomorrow Grandma', was then answered with 'Is it? Well it's mine the day after'.

Grandma began to wander at night and had great difficulty sleeping. She was prescribed sleeping tablets but they soon lost their effect. Most days began with an accusation of something having been robbed on her, her post, clothes, shoes, handbag, biscuits, laxatives and even mothballs! Within a few months she began to have falls and it was, after one such fall, that she suffered a stroke and was admitted to hospital. She hardly recognised any of us by then and passed away to join her husband and many children in the eternal garden, she fervently believed was called heaven.

Grandma's death left my mother feeling isolated and very much alone. Both her parents were now gone and her only living sisters far away, busy living their lives, in America. She had her fill of death and loss. She coped as her own mother had, by building her world and focus around her children and so she immersed herself in the rearing of her family.

Chapter 5

Alzheimer's began to carve its devious way into my Mother's life well before she was formally diagnosed. Forgetting where she left her keys and purse became a regular occurrence, so regular that we got used to it and in any case things always turned up. Every Friday my Mother and Father would go to the bank and go shopping afterwards. Banking was a ferociously private matter between them as they each had their own accounts. So Mammy would go in first and Daddy would wait for her in the car. It became embarrassingly awkward that on more than one occasion she came out of the bank and got into the wrong car. She would ring and tell me of her mortification. We would try to laugh it off by visualising the look on the unsuspecting drivers face as Mammy hopped into his car and closed the door firmly. Before the crimson began to rise she would calmly open the door and make her escape. I used to tease her by saying "Mam, why don't you just say that you want to leave Dad? There are other ways to go about it rather than just hopping into the first car you see hoping to head off with a stranger". She always got a good giggle out of that. 'Ooh, you're wicked', she'd laugh.

As the weeks went on I began to notice that she was duplicating the groceries that she already had in the house. She began to double up on everything that she had bought but not used the previous week. Mam always checked her stock before she wrote her shopping list so it was difficult to understand how this could happen. Week after week, butter, eggs, cheese, bacon, and ham would appear to multiply and breed in the fridge until eventually they were past their sell by date and had to be thrown out. "Oh, I'm getting very forgetful, what's wrong with me at all?" became her regular line.

Matters which Mother used to be able to deal with calmly began to cause her great anguish. The forgetfulness was taking its toll. She seemed to over-react to everything, her thinking and reasoning did not appear to be as it was. She became increasingly distressed and annoyed with herself and ultimately incapable of coping with any form of emotional issue. Her confidence sapped the more the doubt in her memory increased.

A few months later, Mam asked me, "Do you think there is anything I could get from the Doctor for this forgetfulness?" "I don't know Mammy but we can see what she says", I replied. And so, the first of many appointments was made and our shared journey into darkness began.

I went into the Doctor with Mam for that first appointment and we discussed the problems she was experiencing. The Doctor performed a memory test there and then and the result was not particularly worrying though memory loss relating to her age was noted. I asked if Mammy could be referred to a Specialist and an appointment with a Geriatric Consultant was requested.

Within three months, Mammy had been seen and assessed by the Geriatrician. Following evaluation of the Mini Mental State Exam along with a poorly coordinated clock mam had drawn, his diagnosis concluded that she had Alzheimer's. My greatest fear was confirmed. The Specialist directed,'Your Mother has a rapid form of Alzheimer's and the quality of her life will seriously deteriorate over the next year. I felt as if someone had just stopped time as I anticipated the world of the unknown which was now presenting itself. I remembered conversations I'd had with people whose loved ones had Alzheimer's. "It's a horrific illness, I wouldn't wish it on my worst enemy. It's the saddest thing ever, you need to be so strong. You know the day will come and she won't recognise you, you will sit beside her and it will not register that you are her daughter. It's the living dead, the long goodbye".

I could not contemplate the future, having to face the excruciating thought of looking into my mother's eyes knowing she has lost the knowledge that I am her daughter, as the beautiful warm glow in her eyes flickers and fades carrying her into a lost, unknown and vacuous world.

I recalled all the wonderful times we shared when she was in the fullness of her health. I thought of the trip to the Aran Islands fifteen years earlier. We took the boat to the island and we were lucky enough to have arrived there on one of the hottest days of the summer. I convinced her to join me in hiring a bicycle. She was hesitant and sceptical initially, having not cycled for a long time. Once she tried the bicycle out though she was hooked and we pedalled from one end of the island to the other, that day, stopping only to eat and catch our breaths. We laughed from morning to night. I can still see her bent over a stone wall laughing; she could hardly talk after I refused the offer of a spin on a horse and cart, telling the driver that carts make me sea sick. We took many holidays and breaks together and were never happier than when we were in each other's company. 'There's never any tension when we are together', she often said.

• • •

I didn't want to believe she had Alzheimer's. I remembered my own first day at school; Mam cycled me there and back. It was a wet miserable morning and I can still picture the duck egg raincoat she was wearing. I clung on tightly to her waist, tucking my head in close to avoid the rain. She put her hand back and gave me half a roll of silver mints. I squeezed them in my little hand cherishing them, because she had given them to me, I did not even throw the wrappers in the bin, I wanted something she had touched that morning close to me in this strange place called school I didn't want to let her go when I got to the school gates. I don't want to let her go now.

I avoided visiting her until the unknown became more unbearable than the known. I grieved for her and for my loss. Memories of the strong, intelligent, loving mother I knew seemed to fade further away and this fade was augmented by my absence. I could hardly speak about her without bursting into tears. I felt so helpless, hopeless and bitterly lonely. It does not matter what age you are when a diagnosis like this comes, at every single stage of my life I always wanted and needed MY Mammy. She supported, encouraged and gently guided me through life. She told me she believed in me, that I was to believe in and trust myself. She taught me to treat people with respect. She taught me the joy there is in giving, the delight you can enjoy in doing an act of kindness. She taught me how to laugh and the freedom there can be in being able to laugh at your self. She explained to me the importance of admirable traits such as loyalty and honour.

I remember leaving home on a snow-covered morning in January years ago, to go and work abroad. Mammy stood at the door in her nightdress, the snow was so thick that I couldn't see her by the time I got to the car, but I heard her gentle voice calling out after me 'Whatever you do Catherine, don't ever change' My heart was tearing apart with the loneliness of our separation but her words filled me with pride thinking she must like me as I am, and I never forgot that morning.

Life takes on a different hue knowing the mother that was, may never be again, as bit by bit the beautiful mind is disintegrating and dying away, long before her perfectly strong body even ponders decline. Within the space of a few weeks of the diagnosis, I felt destabilised, thinking that the spine I'd had all my life in my Mother had snapped, and as with the forward curvature which occurs with same, it can become increasingly difficult to breath, eat or sleep properly. My chief support system was rapidly crumbling.

The greatest compliment my Mother could ever pay a person was to call them a 'true blue'. A true blue, in Mother's opinion, was a loyal, honourable, reliable, trustworthy, faithful and loving friend, a pal who never gave up on a person or situation. I was privileged that Mammy referred to me as a true blue on more than one occasion throughout my life. *A true blue never quits, I thought. A true blue would never abandon her mother when she most needs her, a true blue must always keep fighting for the one they believe in.* I kept this mantra close to my heart and gradually over the next few weeks I came to the realisation that my avoidance of facing the inevitable served only to heighten my fear and strip me of my courage and so I decided that the best coping mechanism for me would be to learn as much about the disease as possible. Feeling that if I were armed with knowledge I would fit into a better place in my mother's life and be in a position to help and understand her as we now would take the

● ● ●

road of the unknown together. And so, as opposed to separating myself from my mother I made the decision to separate my Mother from the Alzheimer's. I was hoping to find some truth in the Latin aphorism "scientia potential est." Knowledge is power.

And so I pulled myself back from the dread of the future and began to accept every day with whatever it would bring. I would take Mammy to the shops even though she was losing interest in looking at or buying anything, she would get tired and bored easily. We went out for lunch, Mammy would eat and enjoy every mouthful of the meal that was served, thankfully she still really loved her food. One day we had just left a restaurant after having had a delicious three course meal, and were heading back to the car when Mammy said, 'Will we go in here for some lunch now', as she pointed at a hotel. I thought she was joking until I saw the sincerity in her eyes. My heart sank as I reminded her that we had just eaten. 'Have we, I don't remember', she said, 'I feel like I have not eaten all day'. 'But remember you had the salmon and loved it Mam?' 'God, no I don't remember that at all, are you sure?' 'Of course I am Mammy', 'Oh that's alright so', she said as she hopped into the car.

Chapter 6

True to the Consultant's prognosis, Mammy's symptoms worsened in the months that ensued and then reached a level which I could never have predicted nor prepared myself for. This new level brought with it the aggressive stage. Renovations had begun on installing a new heating system at home, this involved work being done in every room in the house. If we knew then what we know now then the work would never have been commissioned. The constant presence of the plumber in the house, combined with the movement of every piece of furniture almost drove my mother over the edge. She became extremely aggressive and agitated and wanted to physically harm my Father as well as the plumber.

Each day I would go and take her off for a drive while the work was being done, we would return in the evening and I would tidy up and try to get some structure back in the house in order to minimise the distress and disruption already tormenting my mother's mind. The plumbing reconstruction went on for weeks.

One day I took my mother off for a drive through country lanes and rural villages which we had never been to before. I thought a scenic route would prove calming. Poor Mam was still uptight though. The rush of getting ready and out before the plumber arrived that morning left her unsettled. A general debate on a topic seemed to make Mammy get uncharacteristically cross and perturbed. I tried to calm the situation without avail. My instinct told me that I would need help in trying to handle this new level of Alzheimer's. I knew I needed to speak to her GP as soon as

• • •

possible. I pulled up outside the Clinic, and swallowed the lump in my throat. I was not sure if I could even translate what had just occurred.

Mam's Doctor was so understanding and sympathetic of what Mammy was going through. I will always remember her words, 'This is a most difficult and distressing time for your mother, she is trying to fight with and understand what is happening to her. In time as the condition progresses, life will become easier for your mother but, of course more difficult for you and the family' She prescribed Lexapro, advising that it was necessary for the short term. I got back into the car and drove my mother home. She took the Lexapro along with her evening pills and got into bed. I was still half afraid to speak to her for fear of resurrecting the aggression again. I wanted to kiss her lovely head as I watched the sleep come. I knew she needed rest in order to give her poor tormented mind a break.

The next day Mammy seemed a little calmer. The trigger was still there though as work was far from being finished. The aggression slowly receded as the days went by and it appeared that she was coming back to herself a little bit. She was more often calm than not. She still wanted to harm the plumber though but was a little more open to tolerating the upheaval as I constantly reminded her of the warm outcome there would be once he was finished installing the new heating system.

Chapter 7

In autumn of that year I took Mam to a musical that my daughter was performing in. My brother had to keep reminding her all day that she was going and why she was going. One minute she would be excited at the thought and the next it all seemed like too much of an effort. In any case she came and I brought my best friend along to ensure that she would not be left on her own at any stage of the evening. The performance went over her head and she did not seem happy among the crowd. At the interval, my friend sat with Mammy while I went to get tea, then I sat with Mammy while my friend went for tea. Mam seemed quiet on the way home. I only discovered the next day that after I left my Mother home, she turned to my brother and angrily announced, 'Well that's the last time I will go anywhere with her, she left me on my own all evening among a room full of strangers'. I was so hurt when my brother told me what she said but I had to accept that this also was a part of the illness, her perception and recall of the evening was far removed from the truth and the sweet memory was distorted.

A few weeks later I brought Mam for lunch again. On the journey in the car she kept checking her handbag. She would open it, look in at her purse, close it and put it on the floor. Two seconds later she would do the very same again and this continued all the way till I parked the car. We were sitting into a lovely meal when she checked her bag again and announced with tears in her eyes 'Imagine Catherine after all my years I haven't a penny left in the world'. 'What?' I yelped in shock. 'Yes, isn't that sad, nothing left to show after all the years working' 'But

• • •

that can't be right' I replied remembering that I had taken her to the bank some months before to lodge an amount of money as I was aware that she was spending less and less as she was not going out as much. 'Well, you can believe what you like', she said as I reminded her of the bank trip. 'Seventy euros is all I have in the world, go on and look for yourself', and she handed me her bank book. I hated looking into her book as banking was always a very private matter for my mother. 'Do you mind if I check it so', I asked. 'Go ahead, I'm telling you the truth' she said. So I looked at the balance and sure enough the bottom line confirmed a balance of seventy odd euros. I looked back a few pages to see if the cash she had lodged a few months earlier had been recorded and it had, but how had it disappeared? On closer inspection I saw that a specific amount was coming out every month by direct debit. Ok, I thought relaxing somewhat, she must have set up a savings account and does not remember. I pointed out the direct debits to her and said 'See, you must have another account and that is where your money is going into'. 'I do not have any other account', she said. 'Ah you have to have Mammy, I'll have a look for a statement when we get home'. 'Well, I'm telling you I don't.'

The journey home felt very long with Mammy repeatedly restating that she had no money, and I repeatedly reassuring her that she had. I couldn't wait to prove it to her. I found a statement which displayed a healthy balance and showed it to Mammy watching her smile as if she had just won the lotto. She was so relieved for all of five seconds till she said again, 'And imagine that, no money after all this time'. 'But you have, we found it' I replied. 'Did we, where?' So I produced the statement and she was happy again for another short while. This went on till I left and went home myself for the night.

• • •

All seemed to be going well until a few weeks later when my brother rang to tell me that Mammy was very distressed, claiming that she was missing a large amount of money. I raced home to find her bedroom pulled apart with her sitting on her bed, crying into her handbag which was open on her lap. She was extremely upset and traumatised. I did my best to talk her down as she ranted that she had been robbed by one of her own children and needed to call the Guards. I calmed her by saying I would try and find it and that it had to be somewhere that nobody would rob her. She cried and cried until she got tired and went to sleep.

The following day my Father rang me in tears saying that life at home was murder and Mammy was raging about being robbed again. I went back down to find her sitting at the range crying and swearing vengeance on the child who robbed their own mother. 'Get me the phone Catherine I'm ringing the Guards this minute'. 'I'll get the phone,' I said 'but just listen to me first; you know it would be a most dreadful thing to accuse someone in the wrong Mammy'. 'I know it would but what can I do', she said. 'Well if the Guards come the first thing they will have to do is search your room, and imagine if they found it, wouldn't we feel terrible for wasting their time? Why don't you and I go and have a good look before we do anything else?' 'Ok, I suppose you are right', she replied.

I had no idea whatsoever whether she had lost money or not but I hoped that the distraction of looking for it would buy some time and give her a chance to calm down. I started by checking the wardrobe and the pockets of her clothes hanging in there. I found 20 euro in one pocket and 5 in another. 'You see, it's possible to

● ● ●

mislay money too Mammy and wouldn't you just hate to accuse someone wrongly', I said. 'I suppose you are right Catherine, sure I'm getting very forgetful'. She seemed comforted with the notes we had found, and with every garment I took out of her wardrobe I would ask her where she bought it and if she thought she might wear it again. The process took a few hours but by the end of it Mammy was calm and not mentioning missing money. I went home.

The next day I got the same phone call again and off I took to repeat the same procedure of calming her and defusing the situation by helping her to look for the money. By evening time she was tired and had forgotten. Daddy had even suggested giving me the substantial amount of cash she believed she was missing, to place in her bedroom in order to get her back to normal. I did not think this was a good idea because it had the potential to confuse matters more, maybe Mammy had never lost any money and if she had, let it turn up legitimately. After four days of the same aggressive outbursts I knew it was going to take more than searching to get her out of this and so I spoke to her Doctor. Lexapro was prescribed again and after a few more days poor Mammy settled and the aggression waned.

Chapter 8

Mother always took great pride in maintaining her home. An oil cloth was essential for dressing the kitchen table and Mammy would take great time and pride when selecting the next new cloth to cover the table. For weeks after the new oilcloth went onto the table, Mammy would monitor it closely to make sure no one cut bread without using a board or left a hot dish directly onto it. I was delighted to hear her say one day that she needed to buy a new oilcloth. So I seized the opportunity and arranged to pick her up and make a day of it. She wanted to buy a mop as well so Daddy gave her a cheque to cover the cost just before we left.

I had a sinking feeling that the cheque would confuse matters significantly as the day out now also involved a trip to the bank in order for Mammy to cash the cheque. I was beginning to learn that you have to act simply and swiftly when Alzheimer's strikes in order to minimise the confusion already being experienced.

'Where are we going again Catherine?' Mam asked as I closed the car door. 'To buy the oilcloth and the mop Mammy'. 'Oh, that's right; well won't it be nice to have a new oilcloth'. 'Well, it will Mam, but I have to bring you to the bank first'. 'Oh? What have we to do in the bank?' 'You have to cash the cheque Daddy gave you'. 'What cheque?' 'The cheque he just gave you to buy the oil cloth and the mop'. 'Did he? And sure I don't have it now do I?' 'You do Mam; you put it in your bag'. So she took up her bag, looked at the cheque, then put it back in and left her bag on the floor of the car. 'What's this we have to do again Catherine?'

● ● ●

she asked two minutes later. 'We are going to buy the oil cloth and mop Mammy, remember? But we have to go to the bank first' 'What have we to do in the bank Catherine?' 'Cash the cheque that Daddy gave you Mam' 'Did he give me a cheque, well that's a miracle'; she laughed as she pulled up her bag and went looking again for it. The conversation remained the same all the way to town, her poor handbag going up and down from the floor to her lap like a yoyo.

We walked into the bank to find a good queue ahead of us. 'What are we doing in here again Catherine?' Mam asks loudly for all to hear. 'You have to cash the cheque Mam', I whisper. 'What cheque, sure I don't have a cheque'. 'You do, the one Daddy gave you, its in your bag Mammy'. So she takes it out, looks at like she has never seen it before and says 'Well didn't he do well to give me that, it must have hurt him'. 'He did Mammy', I replied watching with defeat as she put the cheque back into the bag. 'What's this I have to do again Catherine?' Mam questions as we move a little forward in the queue. 'Cash the cheque', I respond turning red with embarrassment thinking people will think I am forcing her to cash a cheque!

'What cheque?', she begins again as I head her off and whisper 'It's in your bag, Daddy gave it to you, maybe take it out and keep it in your hand now Mammy we will soon be at the cashier please God'. The cheque comes out and she holds it in her hand and asks 'What's this for again Catherine?' 'The oil cloth and the mop Mammy'. 'Oh are we getting an oil cloth for the table is it, that will be lovely, it's badly needed'.

After repeating the same dialogue numerous more times, we reach the cashier and the famous cheque is cashed. 'What did we

• • •

come to town for again Catherine?' Mam asks as I close the car door, pull across my seatbelt and get ready to drive fast to the department store. 'Well we went into the bank first and now we are going to buy the oil cloth Mam and then we will have a nice lunch'. 'What were we doing in the bank?' 'You had to cash the cheque Daddy gave you to buy the bits you want Mammy'. 'Did he give me a cheque did he? Well, if he did I don't have it now'. 'Well you cashed it Mam and put the money into your handbag'. 'Oh right', she says as she pulls out the cash flicking through it. She plants it back into her handbag straight away and leaves the bag on the floor. About two minutes later she takes up her handbag and begins rooting in it. 'Well would you look at that Catherine', she announces with great surprise. 'What Mammy?' I ask as I see her holding the notes in her hand. 'I'm after finding money here that I never knew I had, isn't that a lovely surprise?' 'Sure that's the money from the cheque Daddy gave you Mam'. 'What cheque?', and off we go again round in circles until we arrive at the store.

I know exactly where the oil cloths are displayed so I guide Mammy directly to that area and ask her to select the one she likes the best. 'Sure we're not getting one today are we Catherine?' 'We are Mam, sure that's what we came in for and Daddy gave you the money'. 'Did he, sure maybe we don't need one'. 'Ah, we do Mam; it will be lovely for Christmas'. 'Well if you think so Catherine, I suppose it would, it will brighten up the place'. Mam is drawn to a nice wine and white cheque cloth and I give the measurements to the assistant. The cloth is cut and we head to the kitchen section to find the first mop I put my hand on. 'Are you buying yourself a mop Catherine?' Mam asks. 'No Mammy this is for you, you wanted one remember?' 'Did I? Sure isn't the one we have grand, won't it do?' 'But you need a mop Mam and sure Daddy gave you the money for it anyway so we better get it'. 'Did he give me money did he, well how did he manage that?' 'Well he gave you a cheque', I have it out before I get a chance to kick myself. 'What cheque?' 'The one you just cashed in the bank Mam'. 'Were we in the bank today Catherine?' 'We were Mammy', I reply shoving the mop firmly under my arm and making for the checkout.

That comes to €49.98 the cashier advises as she begins rolling up the oilcloth. For the first time since we came out there is total silence as Mammy stands smiling at the cashier. 'Oh right, €49.98, that's perfect', I said. Mam is still standing there smiling at the lovely assistant as if the transaction has nothing what so ever to do with her. She takes the bag containing the oil cloth and holds it firmly in her hand. In the other hand she holds her own, tightly shut, for the first time today, handbag. With a heavy heart and a lighter wallet, I take out the money and pay for the oil cloth and mop myself.

Laughter erupted up from deep inside me but I could not let it out. The ordeal of the day, the repetition of questions, the queue in the bank, finding money in her bag, the famous oilcloth and mop and I ended up paying for them. Well, I really had to laugh, what else could I do. 'Now Mam, that's done let's go for a nice lunch', I say smiling in the knowledge that the day's work left her in profit and God love her she earned it.

'Oh it's a good job that's all gone I couldn't eat another bite', Mam says as she drinks back the last of her red wine and pushes the plate away. 'That was a lovely meal, and you ate very little yourself Catherine'. 'Ah I'm grand Mammy, I wasn't really hungry, but I'm delighted that you enjoyed it, it's nice to get out isn't it?' 'Well it sure is, it does me the world of good. What did we come in for again?' So I tell her again about the bank and the cloth and the mop. We get up to leave and I help her with her coat. 'Now where are we going?' she asks. 'Sure I suppose we will go home and put the new oil cloth on the table and admire it Mam'. 'And did we get an oil cloth today?' 'We did Mam', I say holding the hotel door open for her. We cross the road and Mammy tugs at my arm indicating a restaurant. 'Will we go in here now and have a bit of lunch Catherine?' 'But you have just eaten Mam, remember the salmon and lovely vegetables?' I say in shock. 'Did I? Well, I don't remember, and did I like it?' 'You did Mam you loved it'. 'Well that is embarrassing Catherine, I don't remember eating at all, I feel like I haven't eaten a thing all day'. 'Oh you did Mam and you enjoyed it, you were ready to burst after it', I say finding it hard to believe it possible for a memory to fade that rapidly.

We get home and I put the oilcloth on the table. Mammy is delighted with the purchase and can't stop admiring the colours and asking where it came from. 'Well God help the one who puts a mark on that', she warns. 'If I catch anyone cutting bread or putting a hot plate on that I'll skull them'. It seems the prospect of protecting that oilcloth will keep her busy for some time yet, and in the meantime she enjoys admiring it.

My Father phones me a few weeks later to ask if I will come down and help Mam writing the Christmas cards. 'She is not in the form and keeps putting it off', he says. I stock up on cheerful Christmas cards, pens, stamps and a nice bottle of port to warm Mammy and bring about a feeling of Christmas while we are writing the cards. Mam finds it a struggle and loses interest quickly. I write out the addresses one by one and put them in front of her to copy. 'Oh won't you do it Catherine', she pleads after a while of hanging out of the pen. 'Ah Mam, you are doing great, and people love to see your writing on the envelope, it would not mean the same if I do it'. 'Oh I suppose, but feck them anyway they are a nuisance', she says as she continues. 'How do you make an 'R' again Catherine?' So I draw the 'R' on a page in front of her. 'And how's this you make a 'K'?', again I draw the letter in front of her. My phone rings and I take the call, Mam stops what she is doing and waits on me to give her the name of the person next on the list. I see her looking out the window and then it looks like she has begun writing herself. When I finish the call I see that she has been doodling on the new oilcloth, colouring in the shapes on it!! 'Mammy', I say in a rushed whisper 'you're drawing on the good oilcloth'. 'Oh did I do that she laughs, sure you won't tell anyone, it'll come off', as she wets her finger and goes to rub her handiwork off. 'Well if anyone else did that you'd kill them', I said. We looked at each other and burst out laughing.

Chapter 9

The New Year brings more aggression and with it numerous kidney infections for poor Mam. She has taken to sitting on the bed in my young sister's room and crying because she has left home. The room is as my sister left it and holds many happy memories for my Mother. 'There is something about the youngest Catherine, you never forget them and it's hardest of all when they leave. All through life you know you have another one left and coming along, but when that last one goes it just breaks your heart, nothing is ever the same again'.

It breaks my heart to see her sit on the bed and cry. Even when she is in the kitchen, if she sees the bedroom door open she cries for her baby who has naturally and instinctively gone off to live her life.

I begin thinking that if I could change the function of the room, it might make life easier for Mam. I suggest redecorating the room and making it into a guest bedroom. The process takes a whole year, not because of any great volume of work but because it takes time to gently make the recommendation and then try to do a bit of work without her seeing the door open, triggering the huge emotion she feels for her youngest. She can almost sense it when the door is open and she arrives down to sit on the bed and cry. Eventually the job is done and it makes an enormous difference to how Mammy sees and feels. The purpose of the room has changed and Mammy is so proud of how it looks.

• • •

Mam begins to mention kidney infections but the following day she will say she does not have one and that she is fine. Early in the summer she is rushed to hospital by ambulance and admitted with a severe kidney infection. Pain along with the severity of the infection seemed to induce extreme confusion. Yet, she had not mentioned pain to anyone, it seemed as if the pain sensors were not communicating and if they were she had forgotten that they had. 'Ah how are you Mammy', I ask as I reach her bed in the ward giving her a big hug and kiss and planting flowers on her lap. 'Sure there's nothing wrong with me at all Catherine is there?' 'Well you have a bad kidney infection Mam'. 'Do I?' she asks like it's the first she has heard of it. 'I think I'll go home tomorrow, sure I've no reason to be here'. 'But you have to be seen by the Doctor on Monday Mam; you need to wait for him to say if you can go home'. 'Do I? And what day is today?' 'Sunday Mam, sure he will see you tomorrow and you will know then'. A few minutes later Mam asks me 'did you say someone is coming tomorrow Catherine?' 'Yes, the Doctor Mammy'. 'Oh', she says looking completely surprised 'And sure what will I tell him is wrong with me, sure there is nothing wrong with me?' 'Well you have a kidney infection so you can tell him that Mammy'. 'Have I, well I don't think I have, but if you say so, sure I'm only wasting a bed in here, I'd be as well off at home'.

The following day Mam is released and sent home to continue a course of antibiotics. The year progresses and the frequency of kidney infections increase. Since Mammy was taken to hospital we remain vigilant when it comes to her mentioning an infection.

The year flows on with numerous visits to the Doctor. The waiting room of the surgery is becoming a place of great dread for me. I have spent numerous cringe filled moments here.

• • •

Mammy will say exactly what she is thinking out loud, she comments on everyone's appearance along with anything that she sees on the television much to my embarrassment. 'Would you look at the size of that one' is just one example 'she is like something you'd pour out of a jug'. It's like being with someone who has Tourette's syndrome but forgets that they have it. Mam was never this blunt and cruel of appearances before. 'Is that a MIDGET', she shouts as a small man appears on the television screen. 'You'd fit him down your pocket'. All heads turn towards us as I whisper 'Keep it down a bit Mam, you can't really be saying things like that'. 'And sure what's wrong with it, isn't he well able to iron', I look up at the screen to see the man ironing clothes and he barely visible above the ironing board. Please God let us be called very soon I pray.

Two beautiful girls appear next on the TV screen, I think well we should be safe enough here. They are standing under a massive sycamore tree, sun shining brightly above them and before I can draw my breath they begin to kiss. 'Are they LESBIANS?' Mam explodes lifting the other patients off their seats in shock. With little dignity left to lose I sigh, 'Yes Mammy they are'. 'Sure maybe they're right', she said. I think I want to cry when I notice a mixed race couple walk into the waiting room. If there is a God up there at all, please spare me this one. I suppose God met me half way, Mammy said nothing. This time instead she raised her elbow and nudged me sharply in the ribs!

Mammy's name is called out over the intercom and I have her standing before she hardly knows it. I walk briskly down the hall wanting to hide in the Doctor's room and never come out. Not much sanctuary or solace here I discover as I am made feel like a liar. 'Hello, how have you been keeping? What can I do for you

• • •

today?' the Doctor asks. 'Sure there is nothing wrong with me I'm great, never better', Mammy replies. 'Well we think you have a bit of a kidney infection Mammy', I hint. 'Oh I do not. I never felt better'. 'Sure it's no harm to check you out anyway, just to be sure' the Doctor smiles. And so the Doctor checks and confirms that there is an infection present and Mammy is prescribed antibiotics. Not long after she finishes the course of antibiotics the same procedure happens over again. The upside to the many Doctors' appointments she had, was that we got to enjoy many lunches out together, even though Mam was forgetting them with increasing regularity. One afternoon as we were eating lunch a Guard came and sat at the table next to us. A conversation ensued and Mammy kept asking him his name and where he was from, a bit of a reversal of roles was occurring right before my eyes! I know he must have guessed that Mammy had Alzheimer's after she asked him where he was from the tenth time. Still, we had a good chat and Mammy thought he was a lovely fella. She had finished her glass of wine so we got up to go and bid our farewell to the Guard. As we walked out the door I said to Mam, 'Well, that was nice and we had a good chat with the lovely Guard'. 'We did', she said 'and the fecker will probably do us for drink driving out the road'. As we walk down towards the car park, I feel Mam tug my arm again and say 'We will go in here now and get something to eat'. 'Mammy don't you remember we just ate?' I whisper. 'Did we Catherine, where?' So I remind her of the lunch and chat we just had. 'I suppose we did, did we? I feel like I haven't eaten all day'. 'Ah I'll have to go out and get a job just to keep you fed Mammy', and she laughs heartily.

A few weeks later Mam has an appointment with the Chiropodist and I take her. It's a bitterly cold morning and I feel bad taking her out but the appointment is necessary. The prospect of a nice hot lunch afterwards helped get Mammy going. 'Is it you that has an appointment here Catherine', she asks in the waiting room. 'No Mam you have'. 'Have I? And what for?' she quizzes. I tell her and she thinks it's a great idea and badly needed until a few minutes later when she asks the same thing all over again.

'Oh it's great to sit down', Mam says as I hand her the menu. I suggest a hot breakfast and her eyes light up and she leaves back down the menu. The waitress appears and I hope, even though I know, that she will remember what to ask for. She looks blankly at me as the waitress asks 'What would you like?' I look at Mammy nodding my head up and down encouragingly and try to intimate 'A hot ....?' No, nothing comes until I say 'breakfast' myself. 'Oh that will be lovely', Mam enthuses. The waitress writes it into her notebook and dashes off. All the time we are waiting, Mam keeps asking, 'did we order yet? What did I order? What did you order'? The kitchen door swings wide and the racket of noise escapes. The waitress swiftly delivers the piping hot grill of rashers, sausages, tomato, egg, mushrooms and pudding and places it in front of Mam. 'Who ordered THAT?' Mam jumps in shock as she eyes the plate. The poor waitress does a double take and almost drops the second plate in fright. 'You did Mam; we just ordered two breakfasts'. 'Did we?' she asks and she already tucking into it.

I notice that Mam's command of words and vocabulary is slipping. She does not seem to want to engage in conversations much as she finds it frustrating trying to think of specific terminology. She is beginning to have difficulty deciphering words and conversations along with easily losing her train of thought. The disease has made a start on corroding her verbal

• • •

communication skills. It appears as if it is taking longer for her to understand and digest stories, this is manifested in the expressionless look in her eyes. Mammy always loved to read the Irelands Own Magazine and was addicted to crossword puzzles but she does not engage in these activities anymore. She was a great believer in keeping a diary and writing notes to keep up to date with milestones and events. There was always a handwritten note on the table or pinned to the curtain or marks put in on the calendar on the wall. She does not make notes anymore. She has stopped cooking, doing laundry and using the phone. She sits by the range unable to remember who called to visit last. She seeks constant confirmation and assurance of the day's events from my brother who is now her main care giver. She is losing interest in doing the weekly shop; which was something that she always loved to do and got great satisfaction from buying nice food and feeding her family.

Mammy was always a list maker. If I ever needed anything she had it written on a list before the words were hardly out of my mouth .She wrote lists and made reminders for everything, she had a brilliant mind and memory for not only her own duties but for all of the family too. She always enjoyed comedy sketches but got bored if she had seen them already. I can tell her a joke now or show her a clip and she laughs heartily, then I repeat it ten minutes later and she laughs as if it is the first time she has ever heard or seen it.

It is hard to ever imagine your Mother forgetting your birthday. I was hoping this was not the case when I went to visit Mammy with my daughter on the day of my birthday. I knew my brother had probably reminded her but I also knew that less and less was being retained by Mam. I was sitting in the kitchen, silently

• • •

longing to hear her wish me a Happy Birthday. After a while Mammy got up and went to her room. My heart soared when I saw her carrying a beautiful big birthday bag with a ribbon tied at the top. 'Yes', I yelped victoriously inside 'she remembered!' It had nothing to do with receiving a gift; the greatest gift I could have asked for was just that she remembered me. I almost had my hand out to accept the bag as she walked right past me and handed the big shiny birthday bag to my daughter saying 'Now, that's for you love'. I could see the hurt and compassion, in my daughter's eyes as she contritely opened the bag producing soaps, bubble bath and a child's magazine. We all knew enough not to say any more about it and I went home that evening realising we had hit another level in the cruel game of Alzheimer's.

Chapter 10

It is early in autumn 2011. Over the years I have taken Mam to visit her parent's grave, followed by a trip around the village and town land where she grew up. She always shared the history of the area with me and had a funny story to tell about almost every house we passed. The journeys always triggered the memories of her youth and I enjoyed taking her back and hearing her tales of days gone by. Late in August of that year I decide to bring Mammy 'home', as she calls it still.

As we approach the farm she grew up on she can't remember if her home house is still there. I remind her that it was knocked down a few years earlier by the farmer who bought the land and tears well up in her eyes. We get to the gate and she looks in from the car shaking her head, equal amounts of confusion and nostalgia swimming behind her eyes. 'Do you want to get out and look around Mammy?' 'No. I won't bother. Who's this lives here again?' she asks. 'This is where you lived Mammy, remember? The man who bought it had to knock the house to make room for his sheds'. 'Oh I suppose he did', she says. 'Who's this has it again?' And I tell her.

I convince her to get out of the car and walk to the gate, I notice Mam looking around in bewilderment. I know there are flashing memories in her mind but the presence of Alzheimer's has her in huge doubt and it shows in her eyes. It is like she is on a tight rope swaying right towards her memories of the past and left towards oblivion.

The farmer who bought the farm emerges from the shed, smiling as he approaches. He recognises Mammy instantly and has a great welcome for her. 'Who is it you are?' she asks and I remind her of his name and that he bought the land from her. There is a flicker of recognition but it does not last long. We talk for a little while and he asks Mam if she is going to visit her old friend Katie. 'Is she alive?' Mam asks enthusiastically. 'She is of course and is in mighty health, go on up and see her'. We get back into the car and I try to get to Katie's house before Mam has forgotten but I am not fast enough.

'Who was that man, where are we going now'? 'To see Katie Mam, won't it be great for you to meet again after all these years?' As we drive into the farmyard, I notice Katie's son is working on a tractor, he stops and looks up on hearing us approach. I get out of the car and introduce myself and his eyes light up when he recognises Mammy in the car. She has, that blank gaze about her, looking around but taking nothing in. I gently open the door on her side. 'This is Katie's son mam'. 'Who, what, who's this Katie is again?' 'Your friend from years ago Mam'. 'And where is she now is she dead'? 'No she is in the house and this is her son, come on in till we say hello'. She gets out of the car slowly, trying to figure out who this friend is.

We walk into the cosy farmhouse kitchen to find Katie sitting by the fire. Mammy's eyes light up as she breathes emotionally 'Ah Katie, it's you'. Two old friends hug each other tightly as they both tremble with the emotion of the reunion. It is as if seeing Katie in person has transported Mam back to the past and the talk flows about the old days. Katie loved my Grandmother and had a wealth of stories and memories to share. 'I think my mother loved you as much as she loved her own children Katie', Mam

● ● ●

said. Katie smiled and bowed her head whispering 'I think she did alright'. Katie was in the best of health, her son told us and she still went to mass every weekend. Most weeks she still got her hair done and continued to do her own shopping.

Katie had no sign of deterioration either mentally or physically though she was quite a few years older than Mammy. She took great pride in her garden of flowers still. As I sat and listened to the two pals, I got such a strong urge to picture the moment but I pushed my phone back into my pocket thinking to leave them alone. The urge niggled at me again and I had to honour it. 'Do you mind if I take a photo of the two of you Mam and Katie?' I can send you on a copy.' I offered. 'Sure I don't suppose we do', Katie replied. Mam got up and moved over to sit on the arm of Katie's chair, they looked like sisters with Mam's arm around Katie's shoulder. They were both wearing almost identical outfits, a wool skirt, nylon blouse and a cotton cardigan. I captured the moment, not yet knowing how precious it would become.

Katie walked us out when we were leaving and showed us around her garden which was still in full bloom from the summer. You could tell she was proud to show it off as we examined and admired all the different varieties of flowers and plants. Mammy was in heaven with the sea of blooms surrounding her. Katie leaned on the gate of her garden which was alight with colour and vibrancy, to bid farewell as we drove away. As the lifelong friends waved affectionately at each other, the poignancy of the reunion suddenly hit me and a belief which had no foundation what so ever came into my mind that this might well be the last time Mammy and Katie would ever be together.

● ● ●

Two weeks later I read with shock the acknowledgement of Katie's death in the newspaper. Although the feelings I'd had as we parted that day now made sense, I was stunned. I shook as I picked up the phone to call her son. He told me that indeed Katie had been in the finest of health all her life but a week after our visit she became unwell and was admitted to hospital where she later died. 'You know that photograph you took that day Catherine? Well that was the last photograph that was ever taken of our mother. It would be worth more than millions for us to have it'. 'I am honoured to have taken it' is all I could reply.

I broke the news to Mammy and she cried but of course within minutes she had it forgotten. She had the knowledge that she had heard something sad but just could not remember what it was. So the sad news of Katie's death had to be broken over and over and over again. As we had missed the funeral, I made sure to take Mammy to the months mind mass.

'Where are we going again Catherine?' she asked like a child as I put the Mass card into her hand thinking it would help her to remember where we were going. 'To Katie's months mind mass Mam'. 'What? And is she dead? When did she die? Sure I haven't seen her for years have I?' I put the beautiful photo I had taken of the two friends into Mam's hand as I told her all about our visit two weeks earlier. We walked into the small country church and I picked a seat as close to the altar as I could find.

I thought that it might help mam remember why she was there if she could hear the priest mention Katie's name throughout the mass. I was wrong. 'And tonight we pray for the repose of the soul of Katie...' the priest had not finished when Mam said aloud

• • •

'Is Katie here?' All the heads turned as I whispered 'No Mam, this is the months mind for Katie'. 'And did she die?' Mam almost roared. 'Yes Mam, a month ago', I sighed into her ear. The mass continued until Katie's name was mentioned again bringing with it the same interjection as the same cycle commenced. 'And is Katie here?' 'No Mam, this is Katie's mass'. 'And is she dead?' 'She is Mammy'. 'Sure I haven't seen her for years'. 'You have, you saw her a few weeks ago Mammy', but the precious last visit was well forgotten. I bought a silver friendship picture frame, put the treasured photo into it and left it on the mantelpiece to help remind Mammy of one true friendship, decades of cherished memories which should never be stolen by the ravages of Alzheimer's.

Chapter 11

In early December 2011 I make plans to go and help Mammy write the Christmas cards, knowing that this year will be even more difficult than last. Armed with cards, pens, stamps, the seasonal bottle of port for ambience and a heart full of purpose, I glide into the kitchen and kiss Mammy's soft cheek as she sits by the range, her hair standing on her head after her afternoon nap, the faraway look in her eyes in keeping with the expressionless stance. The last twelve months have indeed taken their toll and getting Mammy to copy names and addresses takes three times longer than this time last year.

She is giving up more quickly now and asking me to write them myself instead. She is muddled and confused and keeps forgetting what the task in hand is. Ever wary of aggression setting in, I tenderly try to guide and encourage her and we take several breaks. After each break it is like starting from scratch which is good in the sense that she believes we are just setting into writing the cards and does not remember that she has struggled through the few cards before.

Mam now has only one surviving sister living in New York and we take out an Irish themed Christmas card to write to her. Mam just about manages to write out the shaky words wishing her older sister, a feebly penned Merry Christmas wish from Ireland. It is signed off with love, with love, I reflect, from the sister who never left. I look up and take in the framed photo of Mam and Katie. Mam's sister knew Katie too, I thought, maybe it would be nice to include that photo with the card.

• • •

I suggest it to Mam and she thinks it's a great idea to send the photo but only after I have to tell her the whole story again about Katie dying. I get her to put the picture into the envelope and this time I write the envelope as the address is long and working out how to space the lines would prove too difficult for Mam. I make a list of all the cards we sent and included the fact that we posted the photo and give the list to my brother so that he will be able to reassure and remind Mam after I go home. I know at this stage that within minutes of my departure Mammy has forgotten I was there at all. I cling on to the fact that I know I was there and kissed her curly head before I left.

Mam always stood at the kitchen window waiting for my car to appear at the front so that she could wave me off. She does not do this anymore; her kind face does not appear at the window as it did for all those years when I drove away to the sound of her voice calling out 'Safe Home Now'. There is a great sense of lonesomeness in this for me.

The following morning there is another potential for a flare-up of aggression as Mammy discovers the empty friendship frame and presents it to my brother declaring, with hurt in her eyes, 'Well of all the people, can you believe that Catherine stole the photo that was in here'. 'No Mam, ye sent it to your sister in America', my brother replied with panic rising. 'I did no such thing, she stole it I'm telling you as sure as I'm standing here' It took great persuasion and persistence for my brother to reassure Mammy that I had not stolen the photo and thankfully he had it in writing for proof. The list had proven vital in warding off the aggression in this instance.

The accusations continued all day long with my brother constantly presenting the list and explaining that the photo was sent and was to be reprinted and replaced. Every time he told her the story she thought it had been a great idea but five minutes later Mammy was back reporting the same theft. I had a new picture printed off as quickly as I could and put back into the frame where, as far as I was concerned, it would remain for evermore.

Tobie, the dog has been the pet at home for more than twelve years. She is getting old and is blind in one eye. Mammy loves her and feels so sorry that she is now losing her remaining sight. Tobie is also beginning to lose her hearing and this contributes to the potential for Mam falling over her. Tobie cannot hear who is coming and cannot see them until it's too late so I thought if I get her a hi-vis jacket then at least everyone else in the house will notice Tobie and not trip over her. Mam thinks it's a great idea, and Tobie even seems pleased to have the warmth of a little jacket on her poor aging bones. I brought Pedigree Chum treat sticks for her and she loved them. When I was leaving I gave the treat sticks to Mam asking 'Will you mind these and give them to Tobie when it is time for a treat?'

'What are they again Catherine', she asks. 'Treat sticks for Tobie Mammy; you can give her one anytime you want'. I put on my coat and kissed her goodbye. When I get to the door I hear her call out, 'And can anyone who likes eat these?' I turned around to see her shoving one of the dog treats into her mouth'. 'Jesus, no Mammy', I said as I raced back to take it out of her mouth, 'they are only for dogs'. 'Are they? Sure what harm could they do?' 'You are gas Mammy', I said as I put the sticks away. 'The last thing we need is for you to start barking, now woof woof goodbye'. She threw her head back and laughed heartily and I have to say, so did I. It was not long before my laughter stopped though as I began to consider that this could be a sign of the beginning of her losing impulse control.

We have not had cats around the house for years, but now that Tobie is not out and about as much as he was, there is an abundance of cats sitting on the windowsills. Mammy cannot bear to see any animal cold or hungry so she has taken to feeding the cats. She forgets that she fed them and so just keeps repeating the process of going to the fridge and getting food for them. She takes anything she finds from the fridge, milk, sausages, rashers, ham, and cheese. The fridge is almost always empty and it takes a while to figure out why. She would never have given good edible food to the cats in the past but now she cannot distinguish and just gives them what she finds. It is a vicious circle because the more food she leaves out the more cats turn up and poor Tobie is no longer capable of chasing them away.

I go shopping with Mam and Dad later on that December. My brother and I suspect that she may not be able to continue this routine for much longer. The thought of her not being able to do what she always looked forward to doing every Friday for more years than I can remember, fills me with despair. Daddy picks up the shopping trolley as Mam stands to the side. He holds the list he now has to make himself and makes for the aisles. Every chance Mam gets she hangs onto and rests on the trolley, uncaring of her surroundings. She appears absent from the procedure of shopping and just about manages to follow the trolley around the shop. Daddy prompts her to pick up items but she has forgotten as soon as he tells her.

● ● ●

It is like she is merely floating through the aisles after my father who is pushing a trolley full of groceries that have nothing whatsoever to do with her. It proves difficult guiding her out of the shop through the crowds as Daddy shuffles with an obstinate trolley. I discuss the hopelessness of the shopping trip with my brother and we begin to conclude that this lifelong routine is nearing its end for Mammy. She is even beginning to say that she is not able for the shopping herself anymore. The other side of our thinking is that this is now the only outing she has in the week apart from the numerous Doctors' appointments and we struggle greatly with the prospect of having to let this go.

From forgetting when to stop eating, Mam now forgets that she might be hungry and her Doctor has prescribed vitamin food replacement drinks. Gone is her ability to prepare food and now I am beginning to notice that her eating skills are declining and becoming a challenge. I take Mam out to lunch and notice that her eating habits seem to be slipping as she mushes all the food into the centre of the plate, looking more like she is playing with it than intending to eat it.

Meat, veg and potatoes merge into one big off putting mound on the plate. She is spitting out bits of food and shoving them under the plate, firing bits of meat off and onto the table if she does not like the look of them. When the meal is served to her she is full of praise of how good it looks. She has hardly swallowed a morsel when she starts giving out. 'Look at that Catherine, you wouldn't give it to a dog' 'What's wrong with it Mam you said it was lovely?'

'Well it's the worst thing I have ever eaten, look at it, the meat is tough, vegetables hard and the potatoes cold, fired back at them

• • •

it would want to be' 'Ah, sure you are eating it all the same Mam'. 'Look, look at that' she says as she drags a piece of meat from the centre of the plate, poking it with the knife before sending it flying. 'I'd love to fire it back at her', she announces. Sweat begins to pour out through me as I notice the waitress coming over to us. 'Everything alright? the bubbly waitress enquires. Mam raises her head from the plate in anger and our eyes meet. I turn quickly to the waitress and say, 'Perfect, lovely, lovely, all good here, thanks a million', I say willing her to move on to another table. 'Fired at her it would want to be, straight in between the two eyes she would want it', Mam declares, her lips and nose curling up in disgust. She keeps eating though, every last bite, apart from the bits hiding under the plate, on the table and down her blouse. 'Oh rotten that was, I'll never stand here again', Mam complains as we walk out the door, and I knowing full well that she will have the rottenness forgotten before we even reach the car.

By late December 2011, I sit clinging onto what I feel is left of Mammy, the heat of the range doing little to warm the hope in my heart. Time since her diagnosis has ticked speedily by and her drawing of the clock is becoming more muddled. 'Time nor tide waits for no man' I remember Mam often said. Strawberry Switchblade's eighties hit makes me want to cry.

Just close your eyes and then remember
The thoughts you've locked away
When tomorrow comes you'll wish
You had today

And as we sit here alone
Looking for a reason to go on
It's so clear that all we have now
Are our thoughts of yesterday

If you're still here when it's all over
I'm scared I'll have to say
That part of you has gone
Since yesterday

And as we sit here alone
Looking for a reason to go on
It's so clear that all we have now
Are our thoughts of yesterday

Well, maybe this could be the ending
With nothing left of you
A hundred wishes couldn't say
I DON'T WANT TO

Chapter 12

Christmas comes and goes and the New Year seems daunting. I don't know whether Mammy feels the days long and boring or whether the time flies by in a blur. She is living in a constant state of the present moment and when that moment goes, it is gone forever. Memories from her early years are still there, that is part of the pact with Alzheimer's. You are left with the faraway past but the immediate yesterdays and todays have frozen over.

I watch her winding the tissue in her hands, over and over again as bits fall off and onto the floor. Her eyes are glazed and her face lacks expression or animation. Most of her days are now spent in bed or by the range looking at her hands. I wonder to myself if there is any activity she could engage in that would occupy or stimulate her. I ask her about her school days and she tells me about the little girl Jackie who took her hand on that first day and vowed to be her friend. 'Did you learn to knit in school Mammy?' 'I did Catherine, sure everyone did that time'. 'And do you think you would be able to remember how to knit now? 'Oh I don't know sure I suppose it never leaves you', she replied unenthusiastically.

The next day I produce some brightly coloured wool and knitting needles, pull up my chair beside her and ask 'do you think you would be able to knit a scarf for me Mammy?' She takes the needles slowly, 'how's this you do it again, ah sure I've it all forgotten now, I wouldn't be able'. I watch with bated breath as it comes back to her. She puts up 40 stitches straight away and takes off knitting into the rows as if she had been doing it for years. I remember years ago hearing the click of Mam's knitting needles as she sat by the range making a scarf or mittens for us She was a very talented dressmaker in her day and made the most beautiful dresses for us growing up. I can still picture a pink and white gingham suit she made for me when I was about 8 years old. An A line skirt with pretty pink and white flower buttons running down the centre; it had a matching bolero with short sleeves. It was more professionally made than anything you could buy in a shop. I felt like a princess wearing it, proud, beautiful and grown up. It was for 'good' wear initially which meant it only came out on a Sunday for mass. In time, I was allowed wear it at schoo,l much to the admiration of my teacher and friends. I have loved gingham ever since and the image of that suit will remain with me for ever.

Mam continued to knit and as the scarf got longer I could see her hold it up examining it. Every stitch was perfect; she stayed at it for hours.

A few days later she is still knitting and has made great progress with the scarf. I've bought her a paisley knitting bag and some more wool and darning needles. My brother tells me she seems so content knitting and does not spend as much time in bed. He has to remind her to take up the knitting of course as she forgets she even started, she will ask 'what's this I'm knitting again' 'A scarf Mam'. 'And who's this it's for?' 'It's for Catherine Mam'.

'Well good on you Mam that's beautiful, show it to me', I ask amazed at the perfection of her stitches. 'Who's this I'm knitting for again Catherine?' 'Me, Mam'. 'And will you wear it?' 'I'll wear it with pride Mammy', I reply. 'Oh there's something about

● ● ●

knitting Catherine, I don't know what it is. What's the word? It's something. Ahm, what is it at all, what's the word?' 'Is it therapeutic Mam?' 'That's it' she exclaims, that's the word. I feel happy when I am knitting, I'm thinking of nothing at all only the next stitch. 'Isn't that brilliant Mam, fair play to you? You could start your own business knitting now and sell them'. 'I'd be a long time getting rich', she laughed.

It's so encouraging to see Mam knitting; I feel there is a security in it for her. She is doing something again that she is capable of. It is all in the present and in the moment she is knitting but it calms her mind and soul. She has visible results for the work she is doing. The wool I choose is soft and comforting along with being her favourite shade of blue. It brings focus to her weary mind and postpones the weight of trying to remember all the time. The wrought tissue is replaced by the wool and knitting needles and a welcome change it is.

By the middle of February 2012, Mammy is setting into her third scarf. My partner was sent a YouTube video by his friend and he opened it up and played it for me. It was about a Doctor in Florida whose husband had reached a very advanced stage of Alzheimer's. Dr Newport, a Physician, began to do some research and following her work on memory loss and Alzheimer's, she learned that the medium chain triglycerides found in pure non-hydrogenated coconut oil helped her husband Steve who was diagnosed with early onset Alzheimer's. His clock test improved within a few weeks of taking the oil.

I phoned my brother and told him straight away. We found the information encouraging and decided to start Mam on the oil. On the 23rd February my brother began by putting a teaspoon of the oil into Mammy's porridge every morning. We could never have envisaged the remarkable changes that were about to take place. A week after starting the oil we detected subtle changes in Mammy's mood. A slight improvement we thought. After two weeks of taking the oil we noticed more significant changes and improvements in her mood and general interest in life again. We doubted ourselves, thinking that we were becoming over optimistic. I began taking notes and logged them in a journal which I will reproduce in this book now to give the reader a sense of how things progressed for us.

Chapter 13

08/03/2012
Two weeks after Mam began taking the oil, I suggest taking her shopping with my brother to a city, she has not been to for at least six months. The last time we were there she had no interest in looking at anything and wanted to go home almost as soon as we arrived. We still went into a few shops but in each of the shops we visited Mam made for the nearest seat and sat down clutching her handbag. She looked like a child waiting on instruction to stand up and leave and she kept asking to go home so we left. My brother reminded Mammy every day on the lead up to go shopping and as usual, he prompted her again the night before the trip. On my way home that morning I noticed a missed call from home. I did not bother ringing back as I was nearly there and assumed it was my brother calling to see if I was on my way.

It was early when I walked into the kitchen and I was surprised to see Mammy up and looking bright, dressed in her 'good' clothes and waiting by the range. 'Howya Mammy, you're up and dressed?' 'Why wouldn't I Catherine aren't we going shopping?' 'We sure are Mam and we will have a lovely lunch too'. 'Oh that's the best bit', she smiled. I automatically assumed my brother had woken her up and reminded her of the plans for the day, so I was confused when I heard his car go up the drive and then see him appear at the door. 'Oh, where did you come from?' I asked. 'I got up early and went to the shop', he replied. 'Did you get Mam up before you left?' 'No, she was asleep when

I left'. We looked at each other and then at Mam sitting there fully dressed with her handbag in her lap. 'So why did you call me?' I enquired. 'I didn't call you at all' my brother said. 'But I had a missed call from home'. I did not dare to believe it. 'Did you ring my phone Mam?' 'I don't know', she replied 'Did I?' 'Well I had a missed call from the landline so it must have been you Mam' 'Sure it must have been me so, I was probably ringing to see if you were on the way, but I don't remember now'.

I couldn't believe that she actually picked up the phone, found my number and dialled it', this was hard to fathom because she had gone well past the stage of being able to use the phone. In all of my life since I had left home, Mam would call me almost every day. If she had not heard from me for a day or two she would worry that something was wrong. I lived for her calls and chats as I know she lived for mine. It was another of the great losses I was forced to accept since she developed Alzheimer's.

Not only did she get up on her own and remember the plan for the day, without prompting, she used the phone to see if I was on the way.

We chatted and laughed all the way to the city. Mam did not ask once where we were going. We parked in the centre and agreed that I would walk around the shops with Mammy while my brother went shopping himself. Mam seemed more interested in looking around than she did the last time we were there. I brought her into a big household department store just to see would she show the smallest interest in anything this time. Mammy always loved a good root around a household shop. Dried and real flowers were her passion. Mam took off on her own, heading straight for the flower section. I took my time

* * *

getting to her, wanting to see what grabbed her attention. When I got to her I saw she had selected and put together an arrangement of flowers from all the different vases. She put one back and selected another colour, I could see her look admiringly at them. My heart lifted at the idea that she noticed the flowers, let alone had concentration enough to put them together in a brightly coloured bunch. 'Oh, they are lovely Mammy', I exclaimed. 'Aren't they Catherine? I like the browns and reds together'. 'Very nice', I enthused. 'But sure where would I put them?' she asked. 'Couldn't you put them in the sitting room or the hall maybe Mammy?' I suggested. 'Ah sure the house is full of them Catherine, how much are they anyway?' I told her the price and she threw them down saying 'Well they can keep them for that money, I don't like them enough to pay that much and I having the house full of them'. 'Fair enough Mam' I said laughing at her thriftiness.

We met my brother and enjoyed a leisurely lunch and laugh together. Mam was in great form and really enjoyed the meal. My brother was proudly sporting a new pair of brown leather boots that he'd had his eye on for a while. They came laced in yellow but had a spare brown pair of laces in the box. He lifted up his foot to show Mam the new boots. 'Oh they're lovely' she said squeezing them and feeling the toe to see were they big enough, just like she did when we were children. They are leather aren't they? 'They are', he replied. 'Well good on you, you needed them badly, I hope you mind them, there will be no sticking you now'. 'Oh I'll mind them alright Mammy', he laughed.

I could see Mam was getting tired and I felt the need to rethink the day's events and analyse whether we imagined that she was

• • •

as in tune as she had seemed so we left the city. Not long after we got home Mam went for her daily nap or "Feather field" as she liked to call it. I knew from the last few years that she would not remember the day's events especially after having her nap as she always wakes feeling confused from the sleep. I didn't expect her to even remember I had been there let alone that we had gone shopping. While she was sleeping my brother replaced the yellow laces for the brown ones. He hated the yellow laces.

Mam went to find him after waking from her sleep, the first thing she said was, 'What time did Catherine leave at?' 'About an hour ago Mammy', he replied in shock. 'Well wasn't that a lovely day we had with her', she said looking down at his new boots. 'Oh I see you changed the laces, you were right, the brown ones are much nicer', and she left the room.

09/03/2012

It is Friday again, and time for the weekly shop. Mam gets up and is dressed and ready to go before anyone else. She is holding a little piece of cardboard in her hand. My brother is amazed to see that it is the shopping list, she has written it out herself! She has not done this for a very long time. She is showing an interest in gardening again. Last Spring went by, for the first time ever, without her planting a flower or bud. She pesters Daddy to dig up the flower bed again, which he does.

Mam cooked rashers, sausages and eggs this evening also from start to finish without supervision. She has not cooked or prepared food for quite some time either.

● ● ●

13/03/2012

The following week Mam stuns my brother by asking 'isn't today Tuesday?' She took her medication from the dispenser left on the kitchen table herself. Last December I sat with Mam in the kitchen when Daddy came in and took his pills off the windowsill. As he began swallowing Mam looked at me and said, 'Would you look at all the pills that fella's taking, and here I am not on a pill in the world'. 'Would you stop Mam and you on a load of pills yourself' I laughed in disbelief. 'What? I am not Am I?' 'Ah you are Mammy'. 'And where are they so if I am, I didn't think I was taking anything at all'. 'Look they are here on the table', I said showing her the pill organiser I'd bought two years earlier, with her medication all boxed according to morning, afternoon, evening and night. 'Am I on all those?' she asked suspiciously. 'And what are they for? 'Memory Mammy, blood pressure and cholesterol, and your bones' 'Oh right, and do I take them every day?' 'You do Mam, we make sure you do so don't worry'. 'Oh well ye are great what would I do without ye at all?', she says with relief.

Mammy seems a lot brighter and more cheerful. She is talking about going to a garden centre for bedding plants and asks my brother to remove the two boxed trees at the front of the house so that she can replace them with new ones. Later on that day she asks him to take out the power washer so that she can clean the front path! This is getting scary, I'm thinking. She peeled the potatoes for dinner, and they were peeled perfectly. We used to ask her to do this up until a year ago just to keep her involved but we gave up as we had to go over them again ourselves afterwards. Mammy never left an 'eye' on a potato all the years she was able to make the dinner herself. Mammy made her own bed also today and wants to wash her hair. Her interest in her appearance had been well lost over the last two years and would only wash her hair when she was reminded to and at that she found it a great ordeal. She seems to be retaining memories of programmes she has seen on the television, is beginning to get up earlier, asking questions and worrying about all of her children again. While my brother was at the shop this evening Mam rang him to remind him to get something for the dinner!

15/03/2012

Mam took notice of a new egg opener she had not seen before and was asking to be shown how it worked. She then asks my brother to check the wooden cabin for paint for her, because she wants to paint a wall! Mammy took charge of painting the house, inside and out, every spring of her life. I remember when she would take into a fit of painting. She would be up at the crack of dawn have the curtains taken down and washed before she set into the ordeal. All day long she jumped up and down off the table she used, instead of a ladder. She felt sturdier on the table. The one thing that used to drive her mad was having to come down off the table to put fuel in the fire because, as children, we would forget to do so. 'Oh if I could only be left at the painting', she would sigh 'I'd have it done in half the time. Worse than lazy ye are, not one of ye would think to put a sod in the fire'.

Over the last few years she hasn't even mentioned paint or redecorating, she has not been noticing that a wall might need a coat of paint, she just hasn't been looking. She is becoming interested in the weather forecast again. She lived her life according to the word of the meteorologists. She asked me when are the clocks going forward and when are we going to get the bedding plants. She is filling her own hot water bottle again and remembering that she has it filled.

● ● ●

16/03/2012
Friday shopping again and Mammy is up and dressed with her grocery list written!.

17/03/2012
Mam is up at ten thirty this morning calling Daddy too saying 'Are you getting up at all today?' She cooked a fried breakfast again on her own. She is showing interest in her appearance and not checking her handbag to look for her purse as often as she had been doing.

Prior to her starting the oil treatment she was obsessed with her handbag, when she was out with me, she was picking it up and checking it repeatedly, at home she panicked several times a day looking for her handbag fearing the worst that her purse would not be in it. She is not doing this as often now. We were used to Mammy forgetting about food and that she had eaten. Half an hour after her dinner in the evenings she would be saying she was hungry again. She seems to be able to remember now that she has eaten, as she does not look for food after a meal. There is a different feel about the house I think. I left a skirt for her to fix to see if she would think of it. I did not expect that she would repair the lining as I had mentioned, I did not expect it to be thought of again. She had said she would mend it and went off for her nap. Later on after she got up my brother commented on the skirt thinking I had forgotten to take it with me. 'She did not forget it' Mam said 'Catherine left it here for me to mend'. This time last year she would not even have remembered that I had called let alone recall my request to repair the skirt.

18/03/2012

First thing this morning Mammy asked Daddy to go to the shop and buy the right coloured thread so that she could start working on the skirt.

19/03/2012

Mammy is very busy and lively around the house. She told my brother that she has a lot of jobs to do and that she was letting things slip and not keeping on top of the housework. She remembers what Chicken Kiev's are and wants them for dinner. Out of the blue she will recall a topic or discussion from the day before

20/03/2012

Mam finished knitting the scarf I asked her to do for my brother. She remembered it was for him and went and left it in his room. She started soaking tea towels again this morning and has taken her own medication before anyone gets up. Mammy was always meticulous about hygiene in the kitchen and one of her weekly chores was to make sure she bleached the tea towels at least once a week. She had not thought of doing this for well over a year at least. She is asking to help with the dinner again and peeled the potatoes perfectly. Mammy loves comedy sketches, Brendan Grace and Mrs Browns Boys to name a few. It didn't matter what you put on for her she would double up laughing at the clips and you could play the same one over and over again and it was as if it was her first time seeing it. We put on the same Brendan Grace DVD this evening, after a few minutes of watching it she said 'Ah will you turn that off sure I've heard all those gags before!' Mammy is looking for hand cream in her bedroom; she always used to love to keep her hands soft. She asked me to get her some hand cream in the shop and when I got back she asked if I remembered to get the cream and if I met anyone I knew there. Her interest in local news or people she knew had well diminished. My brother bought her the Ireland's Own to see if her interest in reading had returned in any way. She read it cover to cover, and then read out all the jokes for us, laughing out loud as she went along. She washed two of her blouses today and hung them on the line. An hour later she remembered she had washed them and went to check if they were dry. She is taking up the knitting instinctively herself without being reminded.

22/03/2012

We have been gradually increasing the amount of coconut oil and now Mammy is taking two tablespoons a day. My brother puts it into her porridge in the morning and into a warm dessert in the evening after dinner. Mammy is in mighty form today because she is going to Salthill with my brother. Salthill is a seaside place that holds special memories for Mammy, from her days of ballroom dancing, to taking us there as children and not to mention her penchant for the many casinos it offers.

I can feel her excitement as I talk to her on the phone before she leaves. She sounds full of energy and enthusiasm at the prospect of her day out and a go at the Slot Machines. Shortly after arriving there they head to one of the casinos and she is in awe at the sight of the carousel of machines in front of her. Clutching the coins tightly in her hand she heads straight for the first fruit machine she sees. Perched on a stool she drops a coin into the slot and pulls the lever on the side activating the machine which revolves the three mechanical reels inside. She keeps going until a bell sounds notifying her of a win. A winning combination of fruits land on the pay line and the coins begin to pour out into the drop box at the bottom of the machine. Her eyes light up as the credit meter displays a win of €24. 'I'm not pouring all that money back in now', she said as she headed for the cashier's desk to change her cup full of coins for a note.

Mammy admires the beauty of the sea as they make their way to a restaurant for lunch. My brother finds that she is not speaking as loudly in company now and is engaging in conversation better than she did. I called her that evening and she recounted the day's events with great accuracy. 'Oh the beauty of the ocean Catherine', she said. 'The calming feeling it gave me and the soothing sound of the waves'. Her vocabulary seems to be improving. She is tired after the excitement of the day but thinks to put her hot water bottle in her bed an hour before she hops in.

She put a clean mat on the bathroom floor. She has my skirt mended and left out ready for me to collect tomorrow. Later that night she thanked my brother for taking her to Salthill, telling him that she had great memories of the day.

23/03/2012

It's Friday again and time for the weekly shopping trip. Mammy took a shirt in from the clothes line and ironed it before she went shopping. I join Mam to see how she is getting on and wonder if I will notice any improvement since the last time I went with her. I was stunned as I observed the difference. Mam must have been given entry tickets for a draw last week and she has them all filled out in her own writing with her name, address and telephone number ready to be put into the collection drum. She took off looking for Coarse Cut Marmalade, the Olde Time Irish variety that she always loved, found it and put it into the shopping trolley. I haven't heard her mention Marmalade for years. She often told me about a young lad she knew growing up, poor as church mice, his family were, she said. He had never seen a jar of Marmalade let alone tasted it so he had no idea what it was. It could have been a kitchen utensil as far as he was concerned. Someone mentioned Marmalade one day in his company and rather than let himself down by showing his ignorance he boasted 'Oh yeah, we have one of them at home'.

From hanging out of the trolley with no participation in the selecting of groceries a few weeks ago, she walked up to the deli counter and slowly eyed the varieties of ham on offer, before asking the assistant for a half pound of the Blackey Smoked. Mammy was always very fussy about ham. 'Don't ever let them give you any old ham, pick it out yourself Catherine', was her advice over the years.

Without looking at her list, Mammy remembers the basics like tea, sugar and butter. We move along to the fridges to get milk. There is a promotion on and the company rep hands Mammy a voucher to present at the till to avail of the 50 cent discount. I don't expect that she will remember to present it to the cashier as that is a long way off yet. She is engaging more with other shoppers and speaks to a little boy, asking him his name.

Renovations have been ongoing over the last few months in the shop, which, in itself can be confusing as products are constantly being relocated as the work continues. Mammy asks the cashier if she is enjoying working in the newly renovated shop. I bag the items as they are scanned and can't believe my eyes when Mammy hands the voucher she was given for the milk to the cashier. 'I think I get something off for that do I?' she asks.

• • •

24/03/2012

Mammy is watching the nine o'clock news tonight and asking questions about stories covered. She takes up magazines and is interested in looking through them. The last thing Mam always did before she went to sleep at night was to kneel at the side of her bed and say her prayers. Through the good times and bad she never forgot to either thank God or asks him for help that is until Alzheimer's took hold. My brother stuck his head round her bedroom door to say goodnight to her and there she was on her knees, hands joined in prayer. 'Oh sorry', he said 'I see you are saying your prayers'. 'Ah it's alright', she replied 'I'm just thanking God for all my blessings'.

26/03/2012

Mam is still getting up early, is more active, jolly and alert in the morning as opposed to being vacant and absent. She makes and eats her own porridge and is sitting by the range reading an article about the President, Michael D Higgins wondering how many children he has.

27/03/2012

It's like a light has been switched back on in Mammy. She is lively and in good form, has her blouses washed and hanging on the line. She is curious with regard to what's for dinner and eager to peel the potatoes without prompting. Her interest and love of food is returning. With supervision, she fills up her weekly pill organiser, a far cry from her thinking she is not on any medication.

28/03/2012

Today I am taking Mammy to a garden centre to buy bedding plants. We made this plan about a week ago. My brother reminded of the proposed outing yesterday at lunchtime. Usually he would remind her again at night but he didn't on this occasion. It is hard to believe that she is up and dressed in her 'good' clothes, cooking her porridge when I arrive. There seems to be a consistency in her improvement. Her short term memories appear to be staying with her. As we drive along she is looking out the window instead of reaching for her handbag. She comments on the oats sewn in the fields, is recognising areas and townlands along the way.

At the Garden centre she recognises and remembers most of the names of the shrubs and flowers and asks questions as when best to plant them. 'And Enda Kenny is in China', Mammy commented on the way home. 'Where did you hear that Mam?' 'On the news', she replied as much as to say 'He hardly told me himself!'

29/03/2012

I notice Mammy is sitting up straighter in her chair, she used to be slouched. She is asking more and more questions about things around the house. She initiates conversation now rather than waiting for it to be started. She knows the name of the President and Taoiseach. If I asked her who the Taoiseach was a few months ago she was likely to believe it was 'de Valera'. She notices her collection of coins on the bookshelf and suggests taking them to the bank. My brother has a cold and she is worrying about him and advising him to go to the Doctor, she also remarked that she thinks he has put on weight – he has. She is getting her shopping list ready for tomorrow.

• • •

03/04/2012

Mammy spent the morning ironing and asked my brother to charge her mobile phone. She hasn't thought of her mobile for over a year.

08/04/2012

Mam remembers that I am away on holidays and worries about me travelling. She pulled out her sewing machine today and used it for the first time in at least ten years. She went for her nap and remembered to say she was dreaming about the round steak that is planned for the evening meal.

17/04/2012

I'm sitting at the kitchen table watching Mammy knitting by the fire. Not so long ago she was letting the fire go out, not able to remember that it needed refuelling. My brother walks by and Mammy lifts the lid of the range, coughing loudly to get his attention. He turns around and without saying a word she points at the turf bucket then points into the range. My brother got the turf and laughed saying 'Ah you're making a right butler out of me'. 'I'm only training you to be self-sufficient', she laughed back.

19/04/2012

Poor Tobie is getting older and her sight and hearing has severely deteriorated.. She is in greater danger of being stood on and there is grave potential for her to trip someone up. She is still wearing the hi-vis jacket but I have been trying to think of another way to alert Mammy to her presence in the house. I bought some cat bells thinking at least everyone will hear her now. 'What's that you have there Catherine?' Mammy asks as I string five of the bells together. 'Bells, I got them in the pet shop Mammy, at least you will hear your Tobie now before you see her'. She burst out laughing and said 'Bell the cat, bell the cat oh but who WILL bell the cat?'

The bells brought to her memory the fable which was developed around a group of mice as they discuss their plan to abolish the hazard of a prowling cat. One of the mice suggests putting a bell around the cat's neck so that they are warned of its advances. The plan is approved and commended, until, the question arises as to which of the mice will actually place the bell on the cat. Needless to say there are no volunteers. Mammy laughed heartily remembering the story, the bells worked very well on Tobie as she couldn't hear them herself, but they almost drove everyone in the house mad until they 'disappeared' a few days later.

21/04/2012
Most of the family called today, Mammy cooked and made delicious bacon sandwiches, then called everyone in to eat. She is retaining stories he heard and relaying them back. She has a note written and left beside her bed to remind herself of an appointment she has with the Doctor along with another note reminding her to look for her nightdress. The solid fuel range is cleaned and she wants to make a note of the date so she will know when it is due to be cleaned again.

25/04/2012
My brother mentioned that he thinks he has a tummy bug going to bed last night. Mammy arrived down to him first thing this morning with a cup of tea then a mug of boiled milk and told him to go to the Doctor. She told him to tidy his room! That is a first in a very long time. She thanked him for leaving out her pills for her. She is looking through a promotional catalogue and getting

● ● ●

excited about the time of year and the prospect of buying plants. Mammy's favourite season has always been spring.

27/04/2012

Mammy made a salad for tea this evening, she hasn't made a salad for years and they were a ritual on a Sunday evening growing up. Full up after Sunday lunch, she liked to think of something light for tea, so she would serve up seven beautifully presented plates of salad consisting of homemade potato salad, pickled beetroot, fresh scallions from her garden, tomatoes, cheese, cucumber, lettuce, ham and homemade brown bread. She kept the Heinz salad cream on her person for fear one of us would finish it off and it was only when we were all seated that she would take it out of her apron pocket and slap a helping of it onto each plate, if you were down on your luck that day, your portion might land somewhere between the plate and the table and it was up to yourself to make the best of it and scrape it back onto your plate. She did the same with mustard and YR sauce!

02/05/2012

It is a beautiful sunny day and Mammy sits out in the garden enjoying the heat. She asks my brother to get Ariel in the shop as she wants to wash her clothes. This is something else that she had well forgotten, washing detergent. She had left her washing days behind, but is taking up this chore herself again. Ariel was something else Mammy used to hide in the house in order to spare it. Only for the washing detergent box was too big, it would have been carried around in her apron pocket too. She had no trouble finding alternative hiding places for it though. You could come across a box of Ariel anywhere. Behind the sofa in the sitting room, the bottom of her wardrobe, behind a coat on the hallstand, Ariel could pop up anywhere. She had a terrible fear of running out of washing powder. It had been top of her shopping list all her life.

Fanta was something else Mam would hide in her attempt to make it last and be in a position to share it amongst us, fairly. Mammy has the fairest hand in the world, she could divide a Mars bar into such equal shares, that there was little or no room left for argument. We still did argue though 'He got the end bit Mam, there's more chocolate on that'. 'Well, you'll get it the next time', she would sigh. There was great psychology behind her hiding place for the Fanta though. Where is the last place a child would ever think of looking for a fizzy drink? The washing machine! She got mileage out of that hiding place for a very long time before it was discovered. 'Oh I'm scourged trying to find hiding places', she'd cry.

07/05/2012
I phoned the nurse to get Mammy's blood test results for cholesterol; it seems to be going down since she started taking the coconut oil. It is now at 5.5 which is the lowest it has been in years.

13/05/2012
I promised I would paint the kitchen and told Mammy a week ago. She remembered it herself this evening and asked my brother to help her clear the kitchen so that I could work more easily.

14/05/2012
I arrive at eight in the morning, armed with all the paint, brushes and rollers. I don't want to wake anyone too early and intend being half way through the job before Mammy gets up. She

woke and remembered herself and comes up to the kitchen where I am painting and makes me tea. We have a lovely day working, chatting and laughing with Mammy reminding me of all the times she cycled home to her mother with a can of paint on the handlebar of her bicycle and how the local pharmacist would comment 'Well there wouldn't be a God in it, if you didn't have luck'. 'He was right I suppose Catherine wasn't he?' 'He sure was Mammy, you have benn lucky and you deserve it', I smile, with the sweat dripping off me from the heat of the range and the paint drying before it has a chance to hit the wall.

27/05/2012

Mammy is missing from her fireside chair this evening. My brother looks out the window to see her in the garden watering her newly planted flowers. No prompts, no reminders she must have been thinking about them herself. There is a wild cat sitting on the wall and she spins around giving the cat a quick blast of the hose sending him racing off, then she throws her head back and laughs heartily.

28/05/2012

Mammy has a routine appointment with her Doctor today. I feel confident for the first time in years sitting in the waiting room with her. She is a lot calmer in herself and, as a result, is happy to leaf through the pages of a magazine, smiling and admiring babies and children in the waiting room .

Mammy adores babies and children, but it was like she hadn't been noticing them over the last few years, they were not on her radar. I know her Doctor sees an improvement in Mammy, I have told her about the coconut oil. Mammy is a lot more talkative with the Doctor and is completely at ease laughing and joking with her. 'Lunch now I suppose', Mam says as we leave. 'That's for sure Mammy'. We sit into a lovely meal and spend the next hour relaxing and chatting. It's like having the old Mammy back. She is pleasant with the waiting staff and remembered to leave a tip. She remembered she ate and did not ask to go into another restaurant like she did every other time before this. She is still watering the plants in the garden in the evening all of her own accord.

We have seen so many incredible improvements in Mam over the last three months; we find it hard to believe that the only thing that is responsible for the changes is the coconut oil she is taking. I wonder if we are being over-optimistic and if this reality can last. I phoned her Geriatrician's secretary and brought forward an appointment for him to see and assess Mam. I want to know if she really is as good as we think she is and the memory and clock tests should help gauge the progression of the Alzheimer's since her last visit over a year ago.

The appointment is scheduled for three weeks' time. Early in June Tobie loses her sight completely and is failing in every way. We make the heart-breaking decision to let the vet put her to sleep and her little hi Vis jacket is returned to me. Mammy misses Tobie around the house; she had been with us for well over twelve years. She thinks kindly and practically about it too though, knowing that no animal should ever be left to suffer.

21/06/2012
Mammy has been talking about her appointment all week, getting her clothes ready and reading the hospital letter to see what time it is at. I collect her early and she is in great form. Appointments always added to her confusion and caused great

• • •

anxiety but she is very relaxed to day. 'What's this the appointment is for today Catherine, memory is it?' she asks before we leave. 'It is Mam'. 'Sure it's too much I remember', she laughed. 'Aren't they taking a great interest in me at the same time though? You'd think they wouldn't be bothered with an old bird like me'. 'Why wouldn't they take an interest in you Mam, sure that's what they are there for'?

She settled herself into the car and I notice she placed the handbag firmly between her feet. This is the first time I have seen her put it there, it is normally on the floor to the right, I know because of the hundreds of times she has picked it up and put it down in the past. I can't believe that for the hour of a journey she only picked up her handbag once. 'You ok there Mam?, I ask the one time she picked it up. 'Oh I'm grand Catherine, I'm just checking that I have all my credentials for the Doctor', she replies taking the letter out and reading it again.

I think she put the handbag between her feet so that she could feel that it was there and this eliminated the constant need to check. She did not ask where we were going once during the journey, she didn't have to because she remembered. All previous appointments to the hospital threw Mammy extremely out of sync which in turn amplified the chaos which was occurring in her brain. We arrive at the hospital in good time and I can't get over how in tune and calm she is. 'I'd eat a horse', she whispers to me in the waiting room. 'I can't wait to be done here so we can go for lunch. Where do you think we will go Catherine?' 'Anywhere you like Mam, we will try and think of somewhere different to go this time, somewhere we don't normally go' 'Well I can't wait', she says.

● ● ●

The nurse comes into the waiting room carrying a file and calls out Mammy's name. She hops up before me and we follow the nurse down the corridor and into a room with a young lady Doctor sitting behind a desk. She introduces herself to Mammy, has a brief read of her file and proceeds with the MMSE (Mini Mental State Examination), the tool that is used to help assess the progression and severity in cases of dementia and Alzheimer's by evaluating a person's memory, attention and language. 'Can you tell me the name of the building you are in now? What month do we have? What is the name of the current President of Ireland? She holds up a pen and asks Mam to identify it. Can you name two streets in this city? Listen carefully I am going to call out the names of three items and I will ask you to repeat them again in a few minutes. Ball, box, hammer.' 'Ball, box, hammer, ball, box, hammer', Mammy repeats five times. 'Now I want you to write a sentence on this sheet of paper, write anything at all you like as long as it is a sentence' Mammy took the sheet and wrote 'I like going to Galway'. 'Now I want you to subtract 7 from 100'. 'Ooh I don't know if I'll be able to do that', Mam says. 'Take your time' the Doctor says calmly 'there is no rush'.

'Let me see, 100 take away 7. Ninety three is it?' 'Very good, now subtract another 7 from that' 'Ooh that is hard, let me see ninety three take away seven, eighty six is it?' Well done, and now another seven from that' Mammy thinks hard and is trying to figure it out on her fingers. 'Seventy nine' she says exhaling loudly and I feel like punching the air. I nearly had the calculator out myself trying to think of the answers. 'I mentioned three items earlier, can you repeat them to me now'. 'Oh now what's this they were?' Mammy says scratching her head. She thinks and thinks 'Ball, was one of them ball?' 'It was, very good now the others' 'Ball .... ball........... Box!' 'Excellent, can you think of the last one?' 'Am let me see, no it won't come to me I can't think of it.' 'That's no problem, it was hammer'. 'Oh that's right', Mam says. The Doctor hands Mammy a page with written instruction and asks her to read and follow them.

Mammy read it out 'Take a piece of paper into your right hand, fold it in half then place it on the floor using your left hand, then pick it up and hand it back'. Mammy follows the instruction right away and left the piece of paper on the floor. 'Great, now pick it up and hand it back to me', the Doctor asks and immediately Mam picks up the paper and hands it back to the Doctor. Mammy is then handed a blank sheet and asked to draw a clock and put in all the numbers which she does very well. I feel like the proud Mammy beside her. I get the strongest urge to jump up and hug her.

The young Doctor thanks Mammy, gathers up her papers, puts them into the file and leaves the room. Ten minutes later Mammy's Consultant comes bounding into the room. The last time he saw Mammy was over a year ago during a stage of aggression when she was extremely agitated and confused. 'What's going on here?' he booms doing a double take at Mam. 'This is astounding, you got 25 out of 30 in your memory test and you drew a perfect clock' 'Did I? Mam shyly smiles. I told the Consultant about the coconut oil, I had informed his secretary also prior to the appointment. 'Well whatever you are giving her keep doing it because it's working. This is no longer a woman in decline' he said pointing to Mammy 'She is a woman in her prime. Now off you go and I don't want to see you again unless you are in serious trouble'.

● ● ●

I could hardly take what had just happened in, my heart was bursting with pride, I couldn't wait to phone my brother and tell him the great news.

We head off to four star hotels for lunch. Mammy sits herself down comfortably and scans the menu. 'I think I'll have the salmon, what'll you have Catherine, go on now have something nice I'm paying for this'. 'Ah you're not Mam, I'm getting it'. 'I'm paying for it I said and if you don't let me, I won't come out with you again'. 'Ok so Mam, thanks'. We give the order to the waiter and Mammy remembers that she is waiting on a salmon lunch and looking forward to it too'. She won't shock the waiter this time by shouting 'Who ordered that?', when it arrives. Two steaming plates of salmon arrive with side dishes of carrots, parsnips, broccoli and cauliflower followed by dishes with creamy mashed potato. 'Oh well I enjoyed that more than I have enjoyed a meal in a long time', Mammy sighed pushing the plate away and no bits of food hiding under it for a change. 'This is the life Catherine. It's hard to beat a meal that is served up to you. It's never the same when you have to make it yourself. 'Sure you're not in a rush to go anywhere after this Catherine are you?' she asks remembering that I always collect my daughter from school. 'No rush in the world Mammy, relax here as long as you like. Will you have a desert?' 'Sure why wouldn't I, get a menu and we will see what they have on offer'.

Mammy decides on hot apple tart with cream. I am thinking of going to the toilet but I normally don't when I am out with her, for fear she will think I have left her on her own; the scar is still there from the musical experience when she told my brother I left her alone for the whole night with a hall full of strangers! I see that she is relaxed though so I say 'Do you mind if I just run to the toilet Mam'. 'Why would I love, off you go'. I dash off and make it quick. As I make my way back to the table I see Mammy putting her purse into her handbag and scanning the receipt. 'Did you just pay Mam? 'I did and well worth every penny it was. I gave the poor waiter a tip God love him he nearly took the hand off me'.

I burst out laughing, her tipping days were well gone I thought but now, it seems, they are back. 'Thanks very much for that Mam, it was lovely'. 'Well you're very welcome Catherine, sure too much money I have now and not enough ways to spend it'. A far cry from thinking she had nothing. She praised the salmon meal all the way home, remembering exactly what she had eaten.

10/07/2012

Its Mammy's eighty second birthday. As I arrive I notice all the windows of the house open, a line full of washing hanging on the line. It's like she is back from her holidays and taking charge again. There is an air about the place, a presence that was missing has returned, like going back in time to before she was diagnosed. I brought her a cake and fired it up with candles. She laughs at the trouble I went to saying 'It's trying to forget birthdays now I should be'. Later on that night I look over the photo's I took and compare them with the ones I took this time last year. There is something different about her in this year's photo. Her eyes are brighter and more alive; there is an animation about her. Her expression had lost its meaning, when she smiled it was just from the nose down but now her whole face is lit up again. It is like a light has been switched on. The faraway look is being replaced and she has an illuminated, vibrant and mindful countenance about her.

Mammy's oldest sister still lives in New York surrounded by her seven children and their families. Five of my cousins have scheduled a visit for July this year. They told us of their plans last summer but Mammy has not remembered it since. Out of the blue today she asked me 'When are the yanks coming again'. I can't believe she remembered this, its months since we mentioned it. The five cousins along with their partners and children are taking the trip together and due to arrive in four weeks' time. They can't wait to see Mammy but I have explained that they will have to stagger the visits in order not to overwhelm her. Between adults and children they total a party of twenty two and will hire a bus in order to be able to travel around the country together.

In the days before their arrival Mammy seems excited and is remembering that they are due, asking questions about how many of them there will be and what will she give them to eat and drink and where will we fit them all. My cousin Laurie who is organising the trip suggests letting one family at a time off the bus to introduce themselves to Mammy but not to stay long in order to give them all a chance.

22/07/2012
The big day arrives and Mammy is up and ready for the visitors. In the days leading up to their arrival I feared that at any moment we may have to cancel, that Mammy might suggest it is too much for her. I hope the enormity of it all does not leave her in a state of confusion and agitation. The big bus pulls up outside the house, Mammy jumps up and goes out to greet them. She is like a celebrity; they are all waving from the bus at her. The first family hop off introducing themselves one by one, I watch her try to take in all the faces and I see the light of recognition as she

meets each of her nieces and nephews. 'Oh you're the image of your Mother. I can see your father in you'.

The enormity of meeting so many relatives in such a short space of time does not seem to faze her, but I wonder what she will be like this evening when they are all gone, will she have a million questions or will she remember the day at all?. The cousins invite us to join them for lunch so Mammy grabs her handbag and we set off. I feel like hugging her on the bus, fearing that it is all too much for her, instead I just rub her hand reassuringly joking that it's a great service when you can be picked up by bus from outside your door and we living in the middle of the country!

Lunch goes well and each cousin gets a chance to ask their own individual questions off Mam, what was it like growing up, what was their mother, Mam's sister, like as a child, what was grandma like. She answered every question with clarity and accuracy and, honesty, if she really did not know the answer. We got the bus back home and my cousin Laurie asked if she could come back another day before they returned to the States to take a video clip of Mammy and to show her a message that her mother, mam's had recorded.

When they have gone we sit and discuss the excitement of it all and Mammy is still clear about the events of the day. Mammy had taken out all her old photos to show them and we sit for hours going through the albums again. The following morning Mammy talks about all the nieces and nephews she met, and remembers that Laurie is coming for a visit with her husband. It is much more intimate with just Laurie and I feel she gets great quality time with Mammy, hearing stories about growing up in rural Ireland all those years ago and connecting with tales that her own mother had told her. Laurie produces her phone and plays the video message from Mam's dear sister. The greeting my aunt sends to her sister whom, she has not seen now for over sixteen years, is heart-rending and she finishes by saying 'Not a day goes by that I don't think of you, not a day goes by, oh I think of you every day'. Tears pour from my eyes as I watch Mammy waving back at her sister on the phone, believing, at that moment that she can actually see her.

26/09/2012

I've made an appointment for Mam with the Doctor as she has a swollen vein on her leg. The GP, she usually attends is off, so we end up being seen by her husband who also works in the Medical Centre. Mammy has put the connection together, that this Doctor's father was one of the lads that she and her sisters used to meet up with at the crossroads all those years ago in the 1940's and she tells him the story of how Grandma would come over the road and give them 'the look' sending them scattering in all directions.

Her sister was going out with the Doctor's father before she left for America. A week later Mammy remembers the trip to the Doctor's and how we discussed his father with him, she remembers the reason for her appointment. I told her that I am going to Seville for a few days and she asked me not to forget to bring her back a few oranges.

10/10/2012

The house is so quiet without Tobie, a new dog might energise the atmosphere at home, I'm thinking, so we select a beautiful dog from the pound and I proudly deliver him home. His name is Benny and he brings such life to the house again with his antics.

● ● ●

Nothing is safe around him and he takes delight in taunting Mammy by running off with her slippers, tights, shoes and anything else that he finds in his path. She takes a great interest in his playfulness, his presence stimulates her. She has him spoiled rotten with food and he loves it. Mammy remembers I am in Seville and hopes that I get home safely.

15/10/2012

I brought cooking apples to Mam and asked her to make an apple tart. All her old baking skills are very much alive, I'm thinking, as I watch her kneading the dough, then trimming it neatly around the edges. Later on in the afternoon, I go off to the shop, she does not bother coming so I leave her sitting by the range. She usually goes to bed when there is no one around, but I am delighted when I return to find her sitting by the range reading the newspaper intently. I found an old Christmas cake recipe today that Mammy used and swore by all her life. It came from the back of an Odlum's flour bag. Mammy made and decorated the most beautiful Christmas cakes for us all her life, but she has not made one, for at least ten years or more now. I ask her for the recipe and a bit of advice on how to go about making a Christmas cake. I've never made a cake in my life. She encourages me to give it a go and stocks me up with lots of practical tips so I decide to try it

13/11/2012

Mammy can't stop thinking and talking about making Christmas cakes now. I've promised that I will make one with her after I try it out for myself first. She resurrected two scarves that she knitted earlier this year and has left them out to be delivered to the right people. She has an appointment in the hospital on Thursday and this evening remembers to iron a blouse for it.

14/11/2012

Mam remembers her appointment is tomorrow and wants to know what time I am collecting her at.

15/11/2012

We hit the road for Mam's Echocardiogram. She knows her heart is being monitored today and is calm and relaxed and already asking where we will go for lunch afterwards. The boomerang handbag has settled over the last year and remains on the floor of the car for the duration of the journey. I help her prepare for the ultrasound, making sure she is as warm as possible during the procedure. She hates the cold and shivers when the electrodes are attached, then shivers even more when the ultrasound gel makes contact.

I look up at the monitor as the images of Mammy's heart are captured. That's my Mother's beautiful heart I think, that it may last forever. As the Cardiologist interprets the images, noting a narrowing in one artery, Mammy says 'Sure if it gets worse can't you operate, would it be a big operation and how long would it last?'

We head to a beautiful Abbey for lunch. 'Ah this is the life; this is the best part of the day'. I always link Mam when we walk in case she stumbles. She misses a step on the way in the door and we both trip into reception. Mammy burst out laughing 'they will think we're drunk, Catherine'. On the way down to the basement restaurant there is a statue of a jockey. Mammy raises her hand to him saying 'Hello there how are you?' and nudges me as she bursts out laughing. 'That fella is very quiet, he has nothing at all to say', she giggled. She enjoys the Thai meal, great for trying new foods, then sits back comfortably in her chair and begins to sip her wine. 'Sure we are in no hurry anywhere Catherine are we?' 'No hurry at all Mam' I reply, relishing the time with her as the winter sun breaks through the clouds outside. It pours in the window silhouetting her frame and head of beautiful curls.

That is another thing I have noticed since she started taking the oil, her hair is growing much faster and has a lustre and bounce about it, which it hasn't had for years. 'Ooh you have the most beautiful blue eyes Catherine', she gushes. 'I'm as happy here now as I've ever been, I could sit forever' We talked about her growing up again and about Granda and Grandma. 'Think is there a heaven Catherine and will I ever meet them again?' she wonders. 'I hope there is Mam and if you get there before me you're to come back and tell me what it's like' 'I can honestly say Catherine that if I were called this minute I wouldn't have a regret in the world. I've lived my life as best I could, never doing harm, only trying to do good. I stood by and looked after my parents and I have reared five beautiful children. No, I would have no regrets'. 'You're not going anywhere for a long time Mam, we might be reared but we all still need you and I saw a part of you today that you have never seen yourself?' 'What is it you saw?' 'I saw your heart on the monitor, ticking away Mam'. She laughed 'Oh I wouldn't like to have looked at it myself. Isn't it a great organ all the same, ticking away there night and day for what is it, over 80 years and never getting tired'. 'Eighty two years Mam, God bless it' and I raised my glass to her precious heart of gold.

• • •

As we left the Abbey, I asked Mam to take my photo. 'Ah sure I'll cut the head off you like I've always done', she laughed. 'Have a go anyway Mammy'. She held the camera and took two photos, sure enough I was missing a head in the first but the second one was good. I took her arm which was fortunate because she missed the last step again on the way. 'Ah sober up Mam', I joked. She doubled over laughing heartily on the spot hardly able to straigthen. 'The staff are probably looking out the window themselves now laughing at us', she said. 'They are probably saying those two were drunk coming in here and are worse again going out' and we laughed at the good of it, all the way back to the car.

I saw a note beside Mam's bed earlier that morning. It was a reminder that she needed apples. I stopped at the shop on the way home. Normally she would be so tired after the day that she would not bother coming in, but her eyes lit up at the sight of the bright lights of the supermarket. I felt a glimmer of hope wondering if she would remember she wanted apples, even though she had not taken the note with her. Sure enough, she headed straight for the apples 'Oh good I needed these' she said. She browsed around selecting other treats that took her fancy and headed to the cashier to pay. All the way home she praised the lovely day we had together and told me how much she enjoyed her meal.

20/11/2012

I start into making in my first Christmas cake. I phoned Mam this morning asking her how to line the cake tin and she explains it clearly telling me to keep the side lining high in order to protect the top of the cake from burning. 'I'm sitting here now with my feet up listening to old songs about Ireland and it is just

• • •

heavenly' she laughed. 'The best of luck with the cake, it's a big ordeal really and takes a lot of patience' she said. I feel confident now that she is on hand for advice. Two years ago she would not have thought of the cake again, but two hours later she phones me to see how I got on.

She is delighted to hear it is in the oven. Don't forget to pour brandy over it when it is cold' she advises. 'It makes sense you know'. 'If this turns out well, will you make the next one with me Mam?' 'I will of course', she replies.

26/11/2012
Mam keeps asking when are we making the cake together and tomorrow is the day.

27/11/2012
I arrive early loaded with ingredients and there is great excitement. What I look forward to most is the beautiful aroma of cinnamon around home. I remember cosy winter Saturday afternoons growing up, watching Shirley Temple on the television while Mammy was in the kitchen making the Christmas cakes. That is one of my most treasured memories. Mam is fully involved, grating lemons and reminding me to chop up the cherries. Daddy came back from the shop, 'you must be expecting a famine', she joked eyeing the two loaves of bread under his arm. I went to the shop while the cake was in the oven and when I came back she had a needle threaded and was darning a sock! I make her a hot port and we sit back listening to one of her favourite songs, 'Danny Boy'. Tears trickle down her face 'oh that song always reminds me of my father' she cried. The cake turned out very well and as I drive off she is waving at the window and says, 'Look at that for a beautiful moon.' She

then calls out 'safe home and thanks again for everything'. I smiled to myself with the joy of her being back at the window waving me goodbye.

04/12/2012
Mam asked my brother to phone me to ask do I mind if they tuck into the Christmas cake. 'Why would I mind, it's your cake Mammy, enjoy it'.

05/12/2012
It's time to write the Christmas cards again with Mam. I notice such a difference from this time last year. Mammy is eager to start writing, making sure we have all the right stamps for Europe and the US. She didn't ask once how to make any letter, and she needs very little help. She even thinks to add personal notes to some of the cards. For example, in her card to her sister in America she refers to meeting her nieces and nephews during the year and how lovely it was to finally have met them all.

I brought a soft tray to rest on her lap for writing the cards. Later on that evening I notice that she drew a little Christmas tree on the tray. I put sellotape over it so that it never fades. Mammy is wondering what presents to buy for Christmas!

21/01/2013

Mammy has a routine checkup with her Doctor. Everything reads fine and this pleases us all greatly. Something strikes me as Mammy does up the buttons on her blouse, she is closing each button with just one hand! I remember seeing her do this before, but it was years and years ago. I used to think it was funny the way she could close buttons with one hand while combing her hair with the other. To see her button single handed today is amazing. When she says today that she's great and never felt better she means it and it is true.

The Doctor puts down her pen and studies Mam and saying, 'You really are much better'. Mam's reply is classic. 'Oh they will have to shoot me to get rid of me!

28/01/2013
Got Mam's test results all functions excellent. Cholesterol is now down to 4.6 this is the best it has been for years! The year is starting well and holds the look of promise about it.

Chapter 14

Over the last year the improvements I noted in Mam have continued and stabilised, infections have become few and far between and we got to gather and enjoy many precious memories together over the course of this year. The Alzheimer's diagnosis was a wakeup call for me; the difference the coconut oil has made in Mam's fight against the disease gave me a second chance to appreciate more fully my Mother. I treasure and value every precious moment with her now, more so than I did before the Alzheimer's clock began its foreboding tick

It can never be said that the oil had a placebo effect on Mam because back in February 2012 she didn't even know she was taking it. She used to have it in her hot porridge or creamed rice but now she drinks it straight mocking 'What's this for again? To make my hair curly isn't it?'

Mam is still reading her favourite papers and magazines and the pen is back on the locker beside her bed. Notes and reminders are scattered around again. It is like the veil she wore has been raised and thrown back. Seeing Mammy's countenance ignite again has been comparable to watching someone come out of a deep, deep sleep. She is again doing crossword puzzles before she goes to sleep. She has renewed her relationship with the washing machine.

I remember when Mam got her first automatic washing machine She hesitantly put the clothes in, brought out a little stool and sat watching the drum revolve. She admitted to me years later that the day the automatic arrived was the most depressing day of her life. She said she looked in at the clothes swirling around and truly believed that she would never see them again! She thought it took forever to hear the click of the lock releasing the door of the machine. Mam is belting out recitations and verses of poems, songs and ballads, some of which I have never heard her quote before. She learned them all from Granda.

Mam turned 83 in July and we spent the day together in Salthill. We walked the prom, hit the casinos and relaxed with a delicious meal. In August, Mam asked if I would bring her 'home'. I drove her to where her family home used to live. We parked at the gate and she looked in and cried, 'Oh when I think of all the times I came in and out of that gate in my youth', she said. 'I'd cycle miles on a Sunday to bring groceries out to my mother. I'd feel so guilty if I did not go for fear she was in need. And the pharmacist would see me cycling past and say, 'Well there wouldn't be a God in it if you didn't have luck for the way you look after your parents'. And I suppose I have been lucky have I Catherine? 'You sure have Mam. You have all your family around you and you are getting the best care in the world' 'I suppose you are right Catherine, I have five lovely children, he was right in what he said. I did have luck.'

We drove on and she told me the history of the houses and landmarks along the way. We went to look at the old national school she used to attend. The memories of Miss O'Connor were still alive and niggling Mam. 'Ooh, I'd love to have met that one again after I grew up, just to slap her face for the way she treated us'.

'Isn't it sad to think that there is no one left around of my age Catherine? It's so lonesome to think that they are all gone, pity we wouldn't come across someone even out walking that we could ask questions of or just talk to.' I tried to imagine how Mammy was feeling, a surge of sadness shot through me.

It must be so isolating to feel that all those who knew you are gone, leaving you alone with the doubts of your own recall. 'Sure you never know Mam', we might come across someone yet.

'I want to try and figure out exactly where 'An Ghairdín' is located. Mammy. Will we go and have a look for An Ghairdín? 'Oh do Catherine, I'll show you the place. Sure there are five of ours buried there'. I pull up outside the stone wall, get out and look over the wall. There are farming sheds to the left. I can't see any sign of a burial place. 'Are you sure it's in here Mam?' 'Oh I'm positive but sure it's probably overgrown by now', she replies wistfully. I notice a tractor drive up and turn into the yard where the sheds are.

'I'm going to ask this man if he knows anything Mam'. I walk up to the tractor and introduce myself and ask the man if he knows anything about 'An Ghairdín'. He knows loads, its part of his father's land. He knows of my mother and her family as his own father was a neighbour of theirs. 'Is your Mother in the car?' he asked. 'She is indeed', I replied. He introduced himself to Mammy. 'There are five of ours buried in 'An Ghairdín' you know', Mam states. 'Are there?' he asks and he proceeds to tell us exactly where it is pointing out the location behind a gathering of trees.

My father did work on it some years ago and painted little white rocks to mark where he thought graves were', he said. 'Some people have come back enquiring after loved ones too over the years. It emerges that older children who died of TB were also buried there, there was a taboo with regard to TB or Consumption as it was commonly known when Mammy was growing up because it was considered to be a poor man's disease. 'My father would be able to tell you much more about it', he said. 'But sure your father is not still alive is he?' Mam asked. Sure we knew each other well'. 'He is of course', came the reply 'He is up at the house now, as bright as a button, go on up and see him he will be delighted'.

We pulled into the farmyard of the landmark farmhouse that Mammy cycled past all those years ago. I went to the door and introduced myself while Mam waited in the car. She always considered it rude to arrive at a house unannounced or empty handed. 'Bring your mother in', John insisted. I watched as two old friends embraced at the farmhouse door. 'John threw his arms around Mammy, hugging her tightly as he whispered 'Come in love, come in, you're heartily welcome'. Mammy broke down in tears with the emotion of finding a friend she thought was gone, someone who could share stories of her past.

John told us stories of Granda, ones that we had not heard before. He recalled that Granda had many high trees on his land and wanted to get rid of them. He cycled to the barracks in Oranmore and bought gelignite, carrying it home on the carrier of his bicycle. Like our Lord, he fell three times on the way home. He told John of the terror that ripped through him with each fall, and how he would close his eyes tightly in anticipation of an explosion! He set the gelignite under the trees he wanted to shift,

* * *

watching them shoot into the air, taking what seemed like forever to return to the earth. Mammy laughed heartily at the boldness of Granda and asked questions of John as I sat and listened with my heart on fire with the idea that I really feel like I have taken her home this time.

Granda used to torment young John with challenging historical questions demanding answers the next time they met. Poor John had no great access to books at the time and felt under great pressure when asked for the answer by Granda. Without the time or resources he was forced to reply 'Not sure yet'. Every time Granda cycled past John's house after that he would shout in 'Not sure yet. Not sure yet'.

Mammy and I discussed all the stories again on the way home and laughed at the good of them. Mam struggled in her attempts to recall all she had heard. The emotion of the reunion with a man she believed was long gone was tremendous. The sensation of finding an equal who could retrace her childhood steps with her, was delightful and made her feel secure and in place; the hours of travelling and talking now taking its toll. In her struggle to remember something she sighed 'My brain is deteriorating Catherine, I guess it's had its day'.'Ah you are especially tired this evening Mam, you took a lot in today'.

Chapter 15

04/12/2013

I have planned to take Mammy for lunch today; there is something I want to show her. I walk into the kitchen at home and am delighted to see Mammy is busy taking a wash out of the machine, keen to get it on the line while there is a bit of drying out. The linen already hanging out there would snow blind you with whiteness. She loves her whites to stay white. When she is finished with the line she comes and sits in her chair by the range. I take out her liquid foundation and begin to apply it, her skin does not reflect her age and her hair has great life and bounce to it. I wet the comb to calm her curls a little. 'Don't wet it too much Catherine, its cold out and I don't want to go out with a damp head'. 'Don't worry Mam, I'll dry it with the hairdryer when I'm finished. When the make-over is complete I sit to finish my tea as Mam admires herself in the mirror. 'Any bit of lipstick to go with that? she enquires. I don't know when she asked me for lipstick before. 'I'll let you do this bit yourself Mam, I'm not great with the old lipstick', I said handing her the tube I found in her make up basket. I smile as I watch her pout into the mirror, smacking her lips together with pride when she is done with the application. Out of the blue she bursts into song. 'Lipstick on your collar told a tale on you …' I burst out laughing at the spontaneity of her performance. Mammy always loved singing by the fire, the songs brought tears to her eyes as she remembered her father's favourite ballads. Those songs brought tears to my eyes sometimes too; some of the lyrics were fierce depressing! 'What are you laughing at Catherine?' she smirked. 'You Mam, the way you just launched into that song, you are gas!' She laughed out loud as she put the mirror back on the shelf and replaced the lid on the lipstick tube, giving her lips one final smack.

'Ooh it's lovely to get out on such a nice day', she says, smiling contentedly as we speed off up the road. 'Hard to believe it is December again, this year has flown altogether and the next one will go even faster', she said. 'You're right Mammy, we would be as well to leave the decorations up all year round in future'. 'Ah but you'd get sick looking at them, the novelty would wear off' she advised.

I park up and run to get a ticket from the machine. Mam emerges slowly from the car. 'You ok there Mam, are you finding it hard to get out?' 'No Catherine, not at all I am just being careful not to bang your door off that car beside us'. We link arms, as we always do and proceed to the hotel.

'Anything exciting on the menu', she asks as I hand her the clipboard. 'I'd like chicken today I think'. 'Chicken it is Mam'. I notice her shiver with the cold after taking off her coat. 'Would you not put it back on if you are feeling the cold Mam?' 'Ah no I'm fine, I'll warm up in a bit', she replied. I get up and move over to sit beside her, pushing up close to share a bit of my heat with her, enough to keep her going until the meal arrives anyway.

A big plate of food is presented, tender chicken breast stuffed with black pudding, piping hot carrots, parsnips, cabbage and creamy buttered mash. 'What's that you are having Catherine, it looks nice?' she asks as she tucks into her meal. 'Caesar Salad

● ● ●

Mam' 'Oh well that won't do much to warm you up this cold day'.

After a delicious hot dinner we move to the reception area of the hotel and sit in the leather armchairs beside the newly decorated Christmas tree. The evening has drawn in quickly and the dark winter clouds gather to steal the few minutes of natural light that is left. There is an elaborate white and gold smiling Santa figure to Mammy's left, you can just about see his eyes, his beard must have risen higher from years of being shoved into, and pulled down from an attic. A garland of pine with fairy lights sits on the mantelpiece over a roasting fire.

Apart from the receptionist tapping away on her computer, bobbing her head in tune to the Christmas songs in the background, we have the place to ourselves. The illumination of the lights combined with the subtle hue in the area creates a perfect setting for what I am about to tell my Mother.

'I finished my book Mam', I whispered opening the laptop. 'Oh God, that's right Catherine, you are some girl, I knew you had it in you, I knew there was something big in store for you.' 'What's it about?' 'It's about you Mam'. 'What?' she exclaimed in pride and disbelief before throwing her head back and laughing hysterically. 'What's it called?' 'Thoughts of Yesterday Mam', and I showed her the cover I had designed. 'Oh that's a lovely name and what a beautiful cover, it has something about it that draws your attention and makes you want to read. I explained how when she had become so forgetful with the Alzheimer's she could still remember her first day at school but the thoughts of yesterday were gone. I watched as she read the lyrics of the Strawberry Switchblade song at the beginning. 'That

• • •

is beautiful, very moving and sad' she said. I scrolled down and watched her read what is to be her life story. Tears of sadness slipped from her eyes as she read the paragraph reliving the death of her beautiful little sister. 'Oh I can't believe you remembered all this, you have captured it so well and it's so accurate and truthful. Where did you get it from Catherine?' From you Mammy, for all the years you sat by the range telling us stories, I remembered them all. I knew I would put them into a book someday'. 'You are something else, you are a genius do you know that?' she praised. 'You know your Grandfather was very clever and teachers once came from a college in Dublin to convince his parents to let him go and further his education. They saw he had potential, but he was the oldest boy and his parents refused the offer as they needed him for the farm'. 'You're Grandfather would be so proud of you now'. I could see the glare of the screen was tiring on her eyes so I pulled my chair up close to her and breathed 'Sit back there and relax, I'll read the rest for you Mammy, and I whispered the chapters of her life into her sweet ear.

On the way home that evening Mammy got so excited thinking about the book and asking what do I have to do next, how the editing and selling process will work. 'Fair play to you, you deserve great credit. I will pray fervently for your success. I've poor Don Bosco damned and tormented asking for favours down through the years. You have great guts Catherine, I am so proud of you. I really am. Ooh that has me all excited now', she gushed.

• • •

So this last paragraph goes to you Mammy. Thank you for sharing your past with me. Thank you for being my present. Your life to me is a priceless gift. I hope you accept these 'Thoughts of Yesterday' as my gift back to you. No matter what happens now, you will go on forever in this book. And so, for fear the fog of Alzheimer's ascends between us again, for fear I lose you while you are living, rest easy in the knowledge that your life now nestles between these precious pages. Know that I love you and will treasure this love till the far end of time.

THE END

Publisher Information

Book Hub Publishing
Book Hub Publishing is an independent book publishing and editing service located in the west of Ireland and you may find us at www.bookhub4u.ie. Why not join a family of national and international authors who have published with us.

Book Hub Publishing's Professional Services team is equipped with an array of first class editors, designers, writers and marketers with experience in the publishing industry. Whether you choose a publishing package, marketing package or individual service, you can be assured your manuscript will be handled with care and professionalism.

Quite simply, we provide quality printing, binding, editing, illustration, cover design and text layout.

• • •

About the Author

The author grew up in the West of Ireland and has had an insatiable ambition to write for as long as she can remember. She wrote short stories as a teenager and always kept a diary. This, her first novel, is biographical in nature, and she has on-going plans to continue with her desire to capture and entertain readers in her own inimitable, humorous way. The idiosyncrasies and whims of the human race continue to animate and energise her and she likes nothing more than to represent them with her own brand of wit and fun

Author's Commentary

With regard to my use of a pen name, can I say that I agree with J K Rowling when she says that a pen name is a writer's best friend? A pen name is liberating and, given the nature and stories contained in this book, I felt it a must to use a pen name. Catherine, being my second name anyway, came easy for me to use

Made in the USA
Monee, IL
02 October 2020